OPPOSING
VIEWPOINTS®
SERIES

Extremism

Other Books of Related Interest:

Opposing Viewpoints Series
The Taliban

At Issue Series
How Should the U.S. Proceed in Afghanistan?

Current Controversies Series
Iran

"Congress shall make
no law ... abridging
the freedom of speech,
or of the press."

First Amendment to the U.S. Constitution

The basic foundation of our democracy is the First Amendment guarantee of freedom of expression. The Opposing Viewpoints Series is dedicated to the concept of this basic freedom and the idea that it is more important to practice it than to enshrine it.

Extremism

Laurie Willis, Book Editor

GREENHAVEN PRESS
A part of Gale, Cengage Learning

GALE
CENGAGE Learning

Detroit • New York • San Francisco • New Haven, Conn • Waterville, Maine • London

Christine Nasso, *Publisher*
Elizabeth Des Chenes, *Managing Editor*

© 2011 Greenhaven Press, a part of Gale, Cengage Learning.

Gale and Greenhaven Press are registered trademarks used herein under license.

For more information, contact:
Greenhaven Press
27500 Drake Rd.
Farmington Hills, MI 48331-3535
Or you can visit our Internet site at http://www.gale.cengage.com

For product information and technology assistance, contact us at

Gale Customer Support, 1-800-877-4253
For permission to use material from this text or product, submit all requests online at www.cengage.com/permissions

Further permissions questions can be emailed to permissionrequest@cengage.com

Articles in Greenhaven Press anthologies are often edited for length to meet page requirements. In addition, original titles of these works are changed to clearly present the main thesis and to explicitly indicate the author's opinion. Every effort is made to ensure that Greenhaven Press accurately reflects the original intent of the authors. Every effort has been made to trace the owners of copyrighted material.

Cover Image copyright Stocktrek/Brand X Pictures/Getty Images.

LIBRARY OF CONGRESS CATALOGING-IN-PUBLICATION DATA

Extremism / Laurie Willis, book editor.
    p. cm. -- (Opposing viewpoints)
    Includes bibliographical references and index.
    ISBN 978-0-7377-4964-9 (hardcover) -- ISBN 978-0-7377-4965-6 (pbk.)
    1. Radicalism--Juvenile literature. 2. Religious fanaticism--Juvenile literature. I. Willis, Laurie.
    HN49.R33E98 2011
    303.48'4--dc22
                                                           2010030779

Printed in the United States of America
1 2 3 4 5 6 7 14 13 12 11 10

Contents

Why Consider Opposing Viewpoints?

> "The only way in which a human being can make some approach to knowing the whole of a subject is by hearing what can be said about it by persons of every variety of opinion and studying all modes in which it can be looked at by every character of mind. No wise man ever acquired his wisdom in any mode but this."
>
> *John Stuart Mill*

In our media-intensive culture it is not difficult to find differing opinions. Thousands of newspapers and magazines and dozens of radio and television talk shows resound with differing points of view. The difficulty lies in deciding which opinion to agree with and which "experts" seem the most credible. The more inundated we become with differing opinions and claims, the more essential it is to hone critical reading and thinking skills to evaluate these ideas. Opposing Viewpoints books address this problem directly by presenting stimulating debates that can be used to enhance and teach these skills. The varied opinions contained in each book examine many different aspects of a single issue. While examining these conveniently edited opposing views, readers can develop critical thinking skills such as the ability to compare and contrast authors' credibility, facts, argumentation styles, use of persuasive techniques, and other stylistic tools. In short, the Opposing Viewpoints Series is an ideal way to attain the higher-level thinking and reading skills so essential in a culture of diverse and contradictory opinions.

In addition to providing a tool for critical thinking, Opposing Viewpoints books challenge readers to question their own strongly held opinions and assumptions. Most people form their opinions on the basis of upbringing, peer pressure, and personal, cultural, or professional bias. By reading carefully balanced opposing views, readers must directly confront new ideas as well as the opinions of those with whom they disagree. This is not to simplistically argue that everyone who reads opposing views will—or should—change his or her opinion. Instead, the series enhances readers' understanding of their own views by encouraging confrontation with opposing ideas. Careful examination of others' views can lead to the readers' understanding of the logical inconsistencies in their own opinions, perspective on why they hold an opinion, and the consideration of the possibility that their opinion requires further evaluation.

Evaluating Other Opinions

To ensure that this type of examination occurs, Opposing Viewpoints books present all types of opinions. Prominent spokespeople on different sides of each issue as well as well-known professionals from many disciplines challenge the reader. An additional goal of the series is to provide a forum for other, less known, or even unpopular viewpoints. The opinion of an ordinary person who has had to make the decision to cut off life support from a terminally ill relative, for example, may be just as valuable and provide just as much insight as a medical ethicist's professional opinion. The editors have two additional purposes in including these less known views. One, the editors encourage readers to respect others' opinions—even when not enhanced by professional credibility. It is only by reading or listening to and objectively evaluating others' ideas that one can determine whether they are worthy of consideration. Two, the inclusion of such viewpoints encourages the important critical thinking skill of objectively evaluating an author's credentials and bias. This evaluation will illuminate an author's reasons for taking a particular stance on an issue and will aid in readers' evaluation of the author's ideas.

It is our hope that these books will give readers a deeper understanding of the issues debated and an appreciation of the complexity of even seemingly simple issues when good and honest people disagree. This awareness is particularly important in a democratic society such as ours in which people enter into public debate to determine the common good. Those with whom one disagrees should not be regarded as enemies but rather as people whose views deserve careful examination and may shed light on one's own.

Thomas Jefferson once said that "difference of opinion leads to inquiry, and inquiry to truth." Jefferson, a broadly educated man, argued that "if a nation expects to be ignorant and free . . . it expects what never was and never will be." As individuals and as a nation, it is imperative that we consider the opinions of others and examine them with skill and discernment. The Opposing Viewpoints Series is intended to help readers achieve this goal.

David L. Bender and Bruno Leone,
Founders

Introduction

> *"What is objectionable, what is danger-*
> *ous about extremists is not that they are*
> *extreme but that they are intolerant. The*
> *evil is not what they say about their*
> *cause, but what they say about their op-*
> *ponents."*
>
> —*Robert F. Kennedy*

Although the word *extremism* is used frequently in political and religious discussions and by the news media, what the term actually means is sometimes unclear. Archbishop Desmond Tutu says an individual behaves as an extremist "when you do not allow for a different point of view; when you hold your own views as being quite exclusive; when you don't allow for the possibility of difference." Extremism is rooted in a system of beliefs that is far from that of mainstream culture, and it allows for little flexibility or tolerance of other beliefs. These beliefs can be religious or political or often a combination of the two.

The American Heritage Dictionary defines *extremist* as "one who advocates or resorts to measures beyond the norm, especially in politics." Note that this definition goes a step beyond merely a belief system—the extremist takes action. That action may be verbal advocacy for his or her point of view or other "measures beyond the norm." Extremist beliefs often result in violence against others who do not share the same beliefs. John W. Gardner, secretary of health, education, and welfare under President Lyndon Johnson, said, "Political extremism involves two prime ingredients: an excessively simple diagnosis of the world's ills and a conviction that there are identifiable villains back of it all." Extremists identify a villain as someone to fight against to further their own cause.

Extremism is often related to strong religious beliefs. In a panel discussion at the International Summit on Democracy, Terrorism and Security in March 2005, Norwegian prime minister Kjell Magne Bondevik summarized the influence of religion on extremism this way:

All religions can be misused by extremists who are seeking to find arguments for persecution or a holy war. History has shown it again and again. We have seen it in Christianity, in the form of the Medieval Crusades, and the persecution of non-Christian and heretics right up to our own times. I am thinking for instance of the so-called Army of God in the U.S. which condones the killing of medical personnel who are involved in abortions.

We have seen it in Judaism; the very expression zealot comes from a group of Jews who used assassination in their fight against the Romans and the Romanization of the Jews. And we see it today in the form of groups such as Khatz, and Chanitri.

And we have seen it in Islam. The word assassin comes from an extremist Muslim sect of the 11th century, which used murder as a tool in their fight against the crusaders and mainstream Muslim leaders.

However, not all extremist groups are influenced by religion; some groups share a common set of values, ideas, and ideology unrelated to religious beliefs. For example, in the United States, many extremist groups are racially motivated. White supremacist movements such as the neo-Nazis and Aryan Nations demonize people of other races. Other groups, such as the Militia of Montana, believe that individuals are not subject to the authority of government. The militia movement is a relatively new right-wing extremist movement consisting of armed paramilitary groups, both formal and informal, with an antigovernment, conspiracy-oriented ideology.

Extremist movements have also formed around ideologies that express ecological concerns and antigay or antiabortion sentiments.

Members of extremist groups may choose to express their extreme beliefs in a peaceful way, or their beliefs may incite them to violent actions. While a relationship between extremism and violence often exists, this relationship is not inevitable.

Since the attack on New York's World Trade Center on September 11, 2001, by Muslim extremists, the word *extremism* has often been used almost synonymously with *terrorism*. However, they are not exactly the same. *Extremism* describes a certain type of belief system, while *terrorism* describes violent actions, usually stemming from extremist beliefs. One definition, from the government of the United Kingdom, says that *terrorism* is "the use or threat, for purposes of advancing a political, religious, or ideological course of action which involves serious violence against any person or property." The U.S. Department of State adds that terrorist violence is "perpetuated against non-combatant targets by subnational groups or clandestine agents, usually intended to influence an audience." In other words, terrorist acts are violent in nature, conducted by smaller groups rather than by a national government as an act of war, and are often perpetrated against innocent bystanders. Since terrorism in general, and Islamic terrorism in particular, is one of the most prevalent manifestations of extremism in the early twenty-first century, many of the viewpoints in this book consider the extremist beliefs behind these acts of terrorism.

The viewpoints in the first chapter consider the relationship between religion and extremism. The second chapter specifically addresses the motivations of Islamic terrorists. In the third chapter, the viewpoints discuss various methods of countering extremism. The final chapter presents several forms of extremism that are being experienced in the United States.

OPPOSING
VIEWPOINTS®
SERIES

What Is the Relationship Between Religion and Extremist Acts?

Chapter Preface

Mahatma Gandhi, a devout Hindu, once said, "Those who say religion has nothing to do with politics do not know what religion is." Gandhi contended that a strong religious belief should inspire a person to take political action in the world. Gandhi took action by organizing a movement of nonviolent resistance against political forces with which he disagreed. His actions could be considered *extremist* in the sense that they were far from the mainstream standards of behavior for his time.

The term *extremist*, however, is more often used today in a pejorative way to describe people whose strong religious beliefs lead them to hurtful or violent acts against those who do not share their beliefs. These extremists would agree with Gandhi's statement that religious belief must also be political, but their actions manifest themselves in a way that is counter to Gandhi's peaceful and nonviolent stance. They feel that they must fight for what they believe in, whatever form that fighting takes—from verbal combat to suicide bombing. Any religious belief can be taken to an extreme and can produce extreme actions. Muslim suicide bombers and Christian Right politicians attest to the correctness of their own religions, and their actions reflect the strength of their convictions.

The Jewish Defense League (JDL) is one example of an organization that emphasizes taking action in response to religious beliefs. This American organization's mission statement includes the need "to advocate, educate and inspire the Jewish people in such notable areas as authentic Torah Judaism, self-defense (including firearms ownership) and security; to vigorously oppose all manifestations of Jew-hatred." One of the group's five principles is "Barzel—iron—the need to both move to help Jews everywhere and to change the Jewish image through sacrifice and all necessary means—strength, force and even violence as a last resort." However, the JDL's Web site also declares that "JDL enforces a strict no-tolerance policy against terrorism and other felonious acts."

Historically, members of the JDL have claimed responsibility for a number of violent acts in defense of the Jewish people, including a 1981 bombing of the San Francisco office of Bank Melli Iran, as well as two other incidents in 1981 where gasoline firebombs were hurled—at the Long Island home of an accused Nazi war criminal, Boleslavs Maikovskis, and at the Egyptian tourist office at Rockefeller Center in New York. The JDL denies responsibility for a 1985 bombing at the West Coast headquarters of the American-Arab Anti-Discrimination Committee that killed Palestinian American director Alex Odeh and injured seven others. But after this incident, a JDL spokesman declared that Odeh "got exactly what he deserved." JDL's policy statements and these incidents illustrate this organization's internal conflict with the question of how, and to what extreme, actions should be taken to support its beliefs.

Returning to Gandhi's statement raises a number of questions. Is it mandatory, as Gandhi claims, for a strongly religious person to take political action? If so, is it possible for a devoutly religious person to take a moderate stand in the political arena, or must his or her actions be extreme? Is violence a necessary part of extreme action, and when should it be forbidden? If a person claims to be religious but takes no political stand, does that mean he or she isn't taking his or her religion seriously enough? These are the types of questions examined by the viewpoints in this chapter.

> "It is undeniably in the world of Islam where—these days—manifestations of religious hatred and terror have been most frequent, most pronounced, most apparent, most consequential, most popular, and most supported by mainstream clerics."

Terrorism Is an Inherent Aspect of Islamic Extremism

Neil J. Kressel

Neil J. Kressel is a professor of social psychology at William Paterson University in Wayne, New Jersey, and has published several books on social psychology. In this viewpoint, an excerpt from his book Bad Faith: The Danger of Religious Extremism, *he discusses what he sees as the dangerous nature of Islamic extremism. He recognizes potential for moderation as well as extremism in Islam, but he gives examples of Muslims considered "moderate" who nonetheless support violence against Jews.*

As you read, consider the following questions:

1. Kressel lists a number of quotes from Sheikh Al-Sudais. Which of Al-Sudais's views leads some to identify him as "moderate"?

2. Which of Sheikh Al-Sudais's views identifies him as "extremist"?

3. Kressel quotes a little girl who spoke on Arabic television about the Jews, calling them "apes and pigs." Why was the woman who interviewed her pleased?

In recent years, observers from a variety of political, religious, and ethnic backgrounds have objected that discussions of terrorism and religious extremism turn too quickly to the Islamic case and then, almost automatically, become mindless and unjustified indictments of one of the world's great faiths. For example, British author William Dalrymple writes: "The massacre of more than 7,000 Muslims at Srebrenica in 1995 never led to a stream of articles in the press about the violent tendencies of Christianity. Yet every act of al Qaeda terrorism brings to the surface a great raft of criticism of Islam as a religion, and dark mutterings about the sympathies of British Muslims." Others have noted that few blamed Christianity when Timothy McVeigh and Terry Nichols bombed the Murrah Federal Building in Oklahoma City in 1995. Similarly, Judaism, Hinduism, Buddhism, and other religions seldom take much heat in the American press when their extremist adherents carry out evil acts. Old habits die hard, some maintain, and Islam has been unfairly singled out for criticism in Western media because of its fourteenth-century history of conflict with Christianity—the principal religion of the Western world.

[Author of comparative religion] Karen Armstrong argues that "[t]he US is the true home of religious extremism" and that "[d]uring the 20th century, a militant piety, often called 'fundamentalism,' had erupted in every major religious tradition. It was a widespread rebellion against secular modernity. Wherever a Western-style society was established, a religious counterculture grew up alongside it, determined to drag God or religion from the peripheral position to which they had been relegated back to centre stage." In her perspective, "[r]eligion itself was hijacked and discredited on 11 September [2001, terrorist attacks on the United States], and it must now be reclaimed by a compassionate offensive which shows that religion can make a difference to a world torn apart by hatred and fear."

The Extent of Islamic Extremism

To some extent, Armstrong is correct. Adherents of many religious traditions felt challenged by the September 11 attacks, and religious extremism is not unique in any meaningful sense to Islam. Yet it is undeniably in the world of Islam where—*these days*—manifestations of religious hatred and terror have been most frequent, most pronounced, most apparent, most consequential, most popular, and most supported by mainstream clerics. To deny this, as Armstrong and other ecumenically minded writers sometimes do, is to deny reality. Moreover, Islamic extremists themselves adamantly insist that their motivation is religious in nature. We would do well to take this claim seriously.

Though many reasonable and tolerant Islamic voices are heard—especially in the West—immoderation coexists throughout the Muslim world and shows up in many forms. Extremists, however they are defined, number far more than a handful and far less than the entire Muslim population. A key—and largely unanswered—question is just how deeply extremism in its various forms has penetrated different Muslim societies across the globe. Equally important, what social, political, and economic forces lend them support; what countervailing visions of Islam stand the best chance of competing successfully; and to what extent have Islamic history, traditions, and sacred texts contributed to the current wave of extremism? Finally, what, if anything, can be done by those outside the faith to support and empower moderates within? . . .

[We] quickly encounter the difficult matter of how to identify moderates and determine which beliefs and actions distinguish them from extreme coreligionists. Let us [consider] the case of a prominent Muslim leader, . . . Sheikh Abdur-Rahman Al-Sudais.

In June 2004, Sheikh Al-Sudais flew to London to inaugurate a large new Islamic cultural center. Several weeks after the September 11 attacks, the sheikh had declared: "It would be a great calamity when the followers of this phenomenon [terrorism] use religion as a camouflage, because true Islam stands innocent from all that. Its teachings stand aloft from people who believe in violence as a course of action and sabotage as a method and bloodshed as a way of reform." And in autumn 2003, the sheikh had urged British Muslims "all to be nice to your neighbours whether Muslim or non-Muslim as the Prophet taught." He further insisted that "Muslims have nothing to do with terrorism or killing innocent people." Thus, it was not altogether surprising when the BBC felt justified in describing the sheikh in sympathetic terms. At the dedication of the London Islamic Cultural Center, the network took note of the religious leader's message that "Muslims should exemplify the true image of Islam in their interaction with other communities and dispel any misconceptions portrayed in some parts of the media." The Associated Press reported Al-Sudais's participation in the event under the headline "Saudi Imam Urges British Muslims to Promote Peace." On the basis of such coverage, one might conclude that this prominent and influential sheikh was just the sort of moderate whom the West ought to support. After all, the online encyclopedia Wikipedia calls him "one of the most widely respected imams in the Muslim world."

Extremism Lurks Behind a Moderate Identity

But Al-Sudais has another, less ecumenical side, one that does not often find its way into English-language media. Just months before his London message, he had sermonized from his home pulpit that Jews are "killers of prophets and the scum of the earth." The sheikh had explained to followers that "Allah had hurled his curses and indignation on them and made them monkeys and pigs and worshipers of tyrants." In this sermon, Al-Sudais proceeded to describe Jews as "a continuous lineage of meanness, cunning, obstinacy, tyranny, evil, and corruption." It was not a new theme for the imam, who in November 2002 had called upon Allah to annihilate the Jews. He further advised Arabs to abandon all peace initiatives with the Jews.

Sheikh Al-Sudais's animus toward Jews becomes even more intense when the Jews he's referring to are Israelis. Around the same time he was leading prayers in London and being hailed by the BBC, the sheikh had praised Palestinian suicide bombers in glowing terms on Saudi television, saying: "You have revived the hopes of this nation through your blessed jihad ['holy war']. . . . With Allah's help, one of two good things will be awarded you: either victory or martyrdom. Our hearts are with you; our prayers are dedicated to you. The Islamic nation will not spare money or effort in support of your cause, which is the supreme Muslim cause."

Additional aspects of the sheikh's worldview may trouble many Americans and others in the West. In February 2004, he lamented that Iraq "bleeds and that the occupant has ransacked it and raped its riches," and he called on Muslims everywhere to unite "to defeat all their occupiers and oppressors," presumably referring to the US forces in Iraq. Though Sheikh Al-Sudais's deepest anger erupts against Jews, he has—on occasion—spoken against Hindus and Christians as well.

Like [Christians] Franklin Graham and Tim LaHaye, Sheikh Al-Sudais believes his own faith is unquestionably superior to all others. He explains that "[t]oday, Western civilization is nothing more than the product of its encounter with our Islamic civilization in Andalusia [medieval Spain] and other places. The reason for [Western civilization's] bankruptcy is its reliance on the materialistic approach, and its detachment from religion and values." He was particularly enraged by one very popular Western-inspired broadcast—the *Star Academy* reality show—which had become the rage of Arab television. The program is an Arab version of the American show *Big Brother*. Young Arab men and women live for months in the same house in Lebanon, though they sleep in separate quarters. Programs such as these Al-Sudais dubs "weapons of mass destruction that kill values and virtue," saying they promote vice and debauchery.

Some who hear the whole story about Al-Sudais might conclude that he is a less-than-perfect poster boy for Islamic moderation, but that he nonetheless possesses moderate tendencies worth encouraging. After all, though he is a foe of globalization, he does not reject modernity altogether. Instead, he suggests that "[t]he collaboration between originality and modernisation [*sic*] does not contradict Islam. We should take from modernisation what benefits our society from a religious perspective and leave what contradicts our values."

More important, and despite his support for terrorism against Israelis, Sheikh Al-Sudais sometimes speaks unequivocally against other manifestations of terrorism, as he did, for example, following the April 2004 bombing of the security service headquarters in Riyadh, Saudi Arabia. He then called on all Muslims to help the police locate the perpetrators of the attack. And when the first phase of the Iraq war was winding down in early April 2003, Al-Sudais spoke of a Muslim "defeat" but also said in a televised sermon that "[t]he bloodshed in Iraq and Palestine must stop immediately.... The killing of civilians, destruction of property, looting, and robberies must all be stopped."

Thus, those who perceive Sheikh Al-Sudais as an influential Islamic moderate are not entirely wrong, but he is certainly not the sort of moderate whom the United States would choose to empower if it had other real choices. It is also true that those who seem more truly "moderate" to Western ears are often unable to command much support in the Muslim Middle East. Thus, in the search for powerful moderates, the West is sometimes tempted to support religious leaders who reflect many of the tendencies observed in Al-Sudais.

Such moderates endorse a general vision of Islam as a religion of peace. They typically condemn the September 11 attacks and disassociate themselves from Osama bin Laden with regard to means, if not ends. Their interpretation of the religious requirement of jihad does not translate into a direct call for violent conflict with the West. They are open-minded about technology and generally are willing to work with the West when common interests exist, though—despite occasional lip service to democratic principles—they typically regard Western culture as despicable and morally corrupt. From a Western standpoint, they show little respect for the rights of women or homosexuals. Separation of church and state is, for them, an entirely alien concept, and few show much spirit for interfaith cooperation, at least in the sense that we often experience it in the United States. Though in principle such Islamist moderates accept Jews and Christians as "peoples of the Book," in practice most are deeply anti-Semitic and show little respect for Christianity. Some view Hinduism with disdain. Most reject the possibility of peaceful coexistence with Israel and view Israel or Zionism as the root of many of the world's problems.

In short, such religious leaders can be classified as moderate only in contrast to others who are even more extreme. But it is a grave error to conclude from this state of affairs that Islam cannot sustain moderate and progressive alternatives to the extremists. All religious traditions, including Christianity and Judaism, can be used to sustain a broad range of positions and ideologies.

Consider in a bit more detail Al-Sudais's description of Jews as "pigs and apes." Not too long ago, an interviewer on an Arabic TV broadcast, *The Muslim Woman Magazine*, queried a three-and-a-half-year-old guest on the matter of Jews. The purportedly unrehearsed little girl announced that she did not like them and, upon further probing, explained that they were "apes and pigs." Asked for the source of this insight, the youngster responded, "Our God . . . in the Koran." No rebuke, correction, or clarification was offered and, at the conclusion of the segment, the obviously pleased adult interviewer declared: "No [parents] could wish for Allah to give them a more believing girl than she. . . . May Allah bless her, her father and mother. The next generation of children must be true Muslims." (This exchange took place on Iqraa, a joint Saudi-Egyptian satellite network that purportedly aims to highlight a "true and tolerant picture of Islam" to refute "the accusations directed against Islam" and to open "channels of cultural connection with the cultures of other nations.")

Thorough Support for Extremism

Sheikh Tantawi, the influential top cleric from Egypt's prestigious Al-Azhar University, would concur with the little girl. So would Sheikh Mahdi, the imam of Gaza City's main mosque; Salim 'Azzouz, a columnist for a major Egyptian daily; Muhammad 'Abd Al-Sattar, the Syrian deputy minister of religious endowment; and many other Muslim leaders.

But the Koranic verses to which the little girl and the learned sheikhs refer are ambiguous. In several places, the Koran does indeed state that some Jews were transmogrified into animals. One section refers specifically to Jews who broke the Sabbath, saying: "You shall be changed into detested apes" (2:65). Another section appears to refer to Jews and Christians, stating: "People of the Book, do you hate us for any reason other than that we believe in Allah and in what has been revealed to us and to others before us, and that most of you are evildoers? ... Shall I tell you who will receive the worse reward from Allah? Those on whom Allah had laid his curse and with whom he has been angry, transforming them into apes and swine" (5:60). Thus, the Koran clearly seems to suggest that *some* Jews were turned into pigs and apes as a form of punishment for perceived transgressions. But, that being said, whether to embrace such statements as a literal message relevant for today is a choice of present-day Muslims.

The Islamic religious tradition provides the extremist with abundant source material.

> *"Not all ... Islamists advocate global jihad, host terrorists or launch operations against the outside world—in fact, most do not."*

Terrorism Is Not an Inherent Aspect of Islamic Extremism

Fareed Zakaria

In this viewpoint, Fareed Zakaria, an Indian American author and journalist, attempts to differentiate Islamists (radical Muslims) and jihadists (violent terrorists). Zakaria contends that relatively few Muslims are jihadists, but many are Islamists. Even though Islamist beliefs seem oppressive to many Americans, Zakaria believes that the United States should work with the Islamists to overcome the violent jihadists, instead of condemning all Muslims as one coherent group.

As you read, consider the following questions:

1. What does Zakaria say about the participation of the Taliban in terrorist attacks in the past ten years?

2. According to scholar Fawaz Gerges, why did the United States win the war in Iraq?

Fareed Zakaria, "Learning to Live with Radical Islam," *Newsweek*, vol. 153, March 9, 2009, pp. 24–29.

3. How does the Washington Institute think tank recommend the United States approach Muslim countries?

Pakistan's Swat valley is quiet once again. Often compared to Switzerland for its stunning landscape of mountains and meadows, Swat became a war zone over the past two years [2007–2009] as Taliban fighters waged fierce battles against Army troops. No longer, but only because the Pakistani government has agreed to some of the militants' key demands, chiefly that Islamic courts be established in the region. Fears abound that this means women's schools will be destroyed, movies will be banned and public beheadings will become a regular occurrence.

The militants are bad people and this is bad news. But the more difficult question is, what should we—the outside world—do about it? That we are utterly opposed to such people, and their ideas and practices, is obvious. But how exactly should we oppose them? In Pakistan and Afghanistan, we have done so in large measure by attacking them—directly with Western troops and Predator strikes, and indirectly in alliance with Pakistani and Afghan forces. Is the answer to pour in more of our troops, train more Afghan soldiers, ask that the Pakistani military deploy more battalions, and expand the Predator program to hit more of the bad guys? Perhaps—in some cases, emphatically yes—but I think it's also worth stepping back and trying to understand the phenomenon of Islamic radicalism.

It is not just in the Swat valley that Islamists are on the rise. In Afghanistan the Taliban have been gaining ground for the past two years as well. In Somalia last week [early March 2009], Al-Shabab, a local group of Islamic militants, captured yet another town from government forces. Reports from Nigeria to Bosnia to Indonesia show that Islamic fundamentalists are finding support within their communities for their agenda, which usually involves the introduction of some form of

Sharia—Islamic law—reflecting a puritanical interpretation of Islam. No music, no liquor, no smoking, no female emancipation.

Extremism Versus Terrorism

The groups that advocate these policies are ugly, reactionary forces that will stunt their countries and bring dishonor to their religion. But not all these Islamists advocate global jihad [religious war], host terrorists or launch operations against the outside world—in fact, most do not. Consider, for example, the most difficult example, the Taliban. The Taliban have done all kinds of terrible things in Afghanistan. But so far, no Afghan Taliban has participated at any significant level in a global terrorist attack over the past 10 years—including 9/11 [September 11, 2001, terrorist attacks on the United States]. There are certainly elements of the Taliban that are closely associated with al Qaeda. But the Taliban is large, and many factions have little connection to Osama bin Laden. Most Taliban want Islamic rule locally, not violent jihad globally.

How would you describe Faisal Ahmad Shinwari, a judge in Afghanistan? He has banned women from singing on television and called for an end to cable television altogether. He has spoken out against women and men being educated in the same schools at any age. He has upheld the death penalty for two journalists who were convicted of blasphemy. (Their crime: writing that Afghanistan's turn toward Islam was "reactionary.") Shinwari sounds like an Islamic militant, right? Actually, he was appointed chief justice of the Afghan Supreme Court after the American invasion, administered [President] Hamid Karzai's oath of office and remained in his position until three years ago.

Were he to hold Western, liberal views, Shinwari would have little credibility within his country. The reality—for the worse, in my view—is that radical Islam has gained a powerful foothold in the Muslim imagination. It has done so for a variety of complex reasons that I have written about before. But the chief reason is the failure of Muslim countries to develop, politically or economically. Look at Pakistan. It cannot provide security, justice or education for many of its citizens. Its elected politicians have spent all of their time in office conspiring to have their opponents thrown in jail and their own corruption charges tossed out of court. As a result, President Asif Ali Zardari's approval rating barely a month into office was around half that enjoyed by President Pervez Musharraf during most of his term. The state is losing legitimacy as well as the capacity to actually govern.

Consider Swat. The valley was historically a peaceful place that had autonomy within Pakistan (under a loose federal arrangement) and practiced a moderate version of Sharia in its courts. In 1969 Pakistan's laws were formally extended to the region. Over the years, the new courts functioned poorly, with long delays, and were plagued by corruption. Dysfunctional rule meant that the government lost credibility. Some people grew nostalgic for the simple, if sometimes brutal, justice of the old Sharia courts. A movement demanding their restitution began in the early 1990s, and Benazir Bhutto's government signed an agreement to reintroduce some aspects of the Sharia court system with Sufi Muhammad, the same cleric with whom the current government has struck a deal. (The Bhutto arrangement never really worked, and the protests started up again in a few years.) Few people in the valley would say that the current truce is their preferred outcome, in the recent election, they voted for a secular party. But if the secularists produce chaos and corruption, people settle for order.

The militants who were battling the Army (led by Sufi Muhammad's son-in-law) have had to go along with the deal. The Pakistani government is hoping that this agreement will isolate the jihadists and win the public back to its side. This may not work, but at least it represents an effort to divide the camps of the Islamists between those who are violent and those who are merely extreme.

American Perspective and Intervention

Over the past eight years such distinctions have been regarded as naive. In the [George W.] Bush administration's original view, all Islamist groups were one and the same; any distinctions or nuances were regarded as a form of appeasement. If they weren't terrorists themselves, they were probably harboring terrorists. But how to understand Afghanistan and Pakistan, where the countries "harbor" terrorists but are not themselves terrorist states?

To be clear, where there are al Qaeda cells and fighters, force is the only answer. But most estimates of the number of al Qaeda fighters in Pakistan range well under a few thousand. Are those the only people we are bombing? Is bombing—by Americans—the best solution? The Predator strikes have convinced much of the local population that it's under attack from America and produced a nationalist backlash. A few al Qaeda operatives die, but public support for the battle against extremism drops in the vital Pashtun areas of Pakistan. Is this a good exchange?

We have placed ourselves in armed opposition to Muslim fundamentalists stretching from North Africa to Indonesia, which has made this whole enterprise feel very much like a clash of civilizations, and a violent one at that. Certainly, many local despots would prefer to enlist the American armed forces to defeat their enemies, some of whom may be jihadists but others may not. Across the entire North African region, the United States and other Western powers are supporting secular autocrats who claim to be battling Islamist opposition forces. In return, those rulers have done little to advance genuine reform, state building or political openness. In Algeria, after the Islamists won an election in 1992, the military staged a coup, the Islamists were banned and a long civil war ensued in which 200,000 people died. The opposition has since become more militant, and where once it had no global interests, some elements are now aligned with al Qaeda.

Events have taken a different course in Nigeria, where the Islamists came to power locally. After the end of military rule in 1999, 12 of Nigeria's 36 states chose to adopt Sharia. Radical clerics arrived from the Middle East to spread their draconian interpretation of Islam. Religious militias such as the Hisbah of Kano state patrolled the streets, attacking those who shirked prayers, disobeyed religious dress codes or drank alcohol. Several women accused of adultery were sentenced to death by stoning. In 2002 the *Weekly Standard* decried "the Talibanization of West Africa" and worried that Nigeria, a "giant of sub-Saharan Africa," could become "a haven for Islamism, linked to foreign extremists."

But when the *New York Times* sent a reporter to Kano state in late 2007, she found an entirely different picture from the one that had been fretted over by State Department policy analysts. "The Islamic revolution that seemed so destined to transform northern Nigeria in recent years appears to have come and gone," the reporter, Lydia Polgreen, concluded. The Hisbah had become "little more than glorified crossing guards" and were "largely confined to their barracks and assigned anodyne tasks like directing traffic and helping fans to their seats at soccer games." The widely publicized sentences of mutilation and stoning rarely came to pass (although floggings were common). Other news reports have confirmed this basic picture.

Residents hadn't become less religious; mosques still overflowed with the devout during prayer time, and virtually all Muslim women went veiled. But the government had helped push Sharia in a tamer direction by outlawing religious militias; the regular police had no interest in enforcing the law's strictest tenets. In addition, over time some of the loudest

Muslim Leaders Who Condemn Terrorism Are Ignored by the Mass Media

I have heard many Muslims reject violence and terrorists as beyond the pale of Islam, calling them "just killers." However, mass media and most Internet sites do not cover this majority voice for they do not deem it as newsworthy when imam [religious leader] after imam rejects violence. As a result, many non-Muslims believe that they do not condemn violence. Indeed, many fairly sophisticated students of terrorism have often asked me why no one from the Muslim community condemns global Islamist terrorism. They mistake the lack of coverage for lack of activity. When I tell them that the majority condemns such action, they seem surprised and say they have never heard a major imam condemn it. However, have just one imam express sympathy for terrorist aims and it hits the front page of the Islamophobic press and is displayed prominently on Islamophobic Web sites. Ironically, the same bias operates the other way, when the most outrageous statements from Sunday morning evangelists in the United States are posted on Saudi Web sites within a day or so, and people in Saudi Arabia believe that these statements represent majority belief in the United States. Sensationalism sells. Editors and producers need to provide more balanced reporting on this issue.

Marc Sageman, Leaderless Jihad:
Terrorist Networks in the Twenty-First Century.
Philadelphia: University of Pennsylvania Press, 2008, p. 161.

proponents of Sharia had been exposed as hypocrites. Some were under investigation for embezzling millions.

An Overlooked Alliance

We have an instant, violent reaction to anyone who sounds like an Islamic bigot. This is understandable. Many Islamists are bigots, reactionaries and extremists (others are charlatans and opportunists). But this can sometimes blind us to the ways they might prove useful in the broader struggle against Islamic terror. The Bush administration spent its first term engaged in a largely abstract, theoretical conversation about radical Islam and its evils—and conservative intellectuals still spout this kind of unyielding rhetoric. By its second term, though, the administration was grappling with the complexities of Islam on the ground. It is instructive that Bush ended up pursuing a most sophisticated and nuanced policy toward political Islam in the one country where reality was unavoidable—Iraq.

Having invaded Iraq, the Americans searched for local allies, in particular political groups that could become the Iraqi face of the occupation. The administration came to recognize that 30 years of Saddam [Hussein]—a secular, failed tyrant—had left only hard-core Islamists as the opposition. It partnered with these groups, most of which were Shiite parties founded on the model of Iran's ultra-religious organizations, and acquiesced as they took over most of southern Iraq, the Shiite heartland. In this area, the strict version of Islam that they implemented was quite similar to—in some cases more extreme than—what one would find in Iran today. Liquor was banned; women had to cover themselves from head to toe; Christians were persecuted; religious affiliations became the only way to get a government job, including college professorships.

While some of this puritanism is now mellowing, southern Iraq remains a dark place. But it is not a hotbed of jihad. And as the democratic process matures, one might even hope that some version of the Nigerian story will play out there. "It's hard to hand over authority to people who are illiberal," says former CIA [Central Intelligence Agency] analyst Reuel Marc Gerecht. "What you have to realize is that the objective is to defeat bin Ladenism, and you have to start the evolution. Moderate Muslims are not the answer. Shiite clerics and Sunni fundamentalists are our salvation from future 9/11s."

The Bush administration partnered with fundamentalists once more in the Iraq War, in the Sunni belt. When the fighting was at its worst, administration officials began talking to some in the Sunni community who were involved in the insurgency. Many of them were classic Islamic militants, though others were simply former Baathists or tribal chiefs. Gen. David Petraeus's counterinsurgency strategy ramped up this process. "We won the war in Iraq chiefly because we separated the local militants from the global jihadists," says Fawaz Gerges, a scholar at Sarah Lawrence College, who has interviewed hundreds of Muslim militants. "Yet around the world we are still unwilling to make the distinction between these two groups."

A More Sophisticated Strategy

Would a strategy like this work in Afghanistan? David Kilcullen, a counterinsurgency expert who has advised Petraeus, says, "I've had tribal leaders and Afghan government officials at the province and district level tell me that 90 percent of the people we call the Taliban are actually tribal fighters or Pashtun nationalists or people pursuing their own agendas. Less than 10 percent are ideologically aligned with the Quetta Shura [Mullah Omar's leadership group] or al Qaeda." These people are, in his view, "almost certainly reconcilable under some circumstances." Kilcullen adds, "That's very much what we did in Iraq. We negotiated with 90 percent of the people we were fighting."

Beyond Afghanistan, too, it is crucial that we adopt a more sophisticated strategy toward radical Islam. This should come naturally to President [Barack] Obama, who spoke often on the campaign trail of the need for just such a differentiated approach toward Muslim countries. Even the Washington Institute [for Near East Policy], a think tank often associated with conservatives, appears onboard. It is issuing a report this week [March 2009] that recommends, among other points, that the United States use more "nuanced, noncombative rhetoric" that avoids sweeping declarations like "war on terror," "global insurgency," even "the Muslim world." Anything that emphasizes the variety of groups, movements and motives within that world strengthens the case that this is not a battle between Islam and the West. Bin Laden constantly argues that all these different groups are part of the same global movement. We should not play into his hands, and emphasize instead that many of these forces are local, have specific grievances and don't have much in common.

That does not mean we should accept the burning of girls' schools, or the stoning of criminals. Recognizing the reality of radical Islam is entirely different from accepting its ideas. We should mount a spirited defense of our views and values. We should pursue aggressively policies that will make these values succeed. Such efforts are often difficult and take time—rebuilding state structures, providing secular education, reducing corruption—but we should help societies making these efforts. The mere fact that we are working in these countries on these issues—and not simply bombing, killing and capturing—might change the atmosphere surrounding the U.S. involvement in this struggle.

The veil is not the same as the suicide belt. We can better pursue our values if we recognize the local and cultural context, and appreciate that people want to find their own balance between freedom and order, liberty and license. In the end, time is on our side. Bin Ladenism has already lost ground in almost every Muslim country. Radical Islam will follow the same path. Wherever it is tried—in Afghanistan, in Iraq, in parts of Nigeria and Pakistan—people weary of its charms very quickly. The truth is that all Islamists, violent or not, lack answers to the problems of the modern world. They do not have a worldview that can satisfy the aspirations of modern men and women. We do. That's the most powerful weapon of all.

> *"Terrorism, we know, is not the exclusive preserve or franchise of dark-skinned, bearded Muslims. But nowadays you might not know it from following the news."*

Terrorism Is Practiced by Non-Muslims

Mehdi Hasan

Mehdi Hasan is a senior editor for the British political magazine New Statesman. *In the following viewpoint, Hasan complains about the minimal media attention that white terrorists receive compared to Muslims or people of color who commit similar acts. He describes a number of white supremacists who have received different punishments than their Muslim counterparts, and he demands that terrorists be prosecuted equally, regardless of race or creed.*

As you read, consider the following questions:

1. Who is Neil Lewington, and why does Hasan think most people have never heard of him?

2. According to the European police agency Europol, what percentage of documented terrorist attacks in Europe in 2007 could be classified as Islamist?

3. How does Hasan compare the punishment given to Islamists and white supremacists?

Imagine, for a moment, that Neil Lewington, who is on trial at the Old Bailey [the central criminal court in England] for preparing for a "campaign of terrorism" using tennis ball bombs, was a British Muslim. The story would be splashed across the front page of every newspaper in Britain, and Sky News would be rolling a loop of images of his scowling, bearded, dark face.

The reality, however, is that you've probably never heard of Lewington (who denies all eight charges of terrorism) because he is not Muslim, or black, or of Asian origin. He is white. And our gloriously impartial, truth-seeking, "colour-blind" media don't seem to care. The coverage of the Lewington trial has been negligible—a few short stories buried deep inside a handful of newspapers, but, as I write, no rolling coverage on Sky News, and not a peep on the main BBC news bulletins or on *Newsnight*.

One veteran home affairs correspondent told me he had asked his editors why the Lewington trial wasn't being covered. "They didn't want to hear about it," he said. "They just weren't interested. It's outrageous."

A Series of Forgotten Terrorists

Lewington is only the latest in a long line of white terror suspects who have "disappeared" from the mainstream media. Have you heard of Robert Cottage? He is the former British National Party candidate jailed in July 2007 for possessing explosive chemicals in his home—described by police at the time of his arrest as the largest amount of chemical explosives of its type ever found in this country. The national coverage of Cottage's arrest in October 2006 amounted to exactly 56 words in a single "news in brief" item in the *Sunday Times*.

There is, too, the case of Martyn Gilleard, the Nazi sympathiser jailed in June 2008 after police found nail bombs, bullets, swords, axes and knives in his flat, as well as a note in which he had written, "I am so sick and tired of hearing nationalists talk of killing Muslims, of blowing up mosques, of fighting back. Only to see these acts of resistance fail to appear. The time has come to stop the talk and start to act." What about Nathan Worrell? This neo-Nazi, described by police as a "dangerous individual", hoarded bomb-making materials in his home, and was found guilty in December 2008 of possessing material for terrorist purposes and for racially aggravated harassment. His trial attracted two passing references in the popular national press, in the *Daily Star* and the *Sun*. And in February this year [2009], not a single national newspaper reported on the self-professed racist Neil MacGregor's guilty plea to threatening to blow up Glasgow Central Mosque and behead a Muslim every week until every mosque in Scotland was closed.

It is as if these crimes had never happened. For most British journalists today, the idea of non-Muslim terrorism perpetrated by non-Irish white folk is inconceivable. Why? Because too many of them reflexively subscribe to the notion that maybe not all Muslims are terrorists, but certainly all terrorists are Muslims.

The Response to White Terrorism

Figures compiled by Europol, the European police agency, suggest that the threat of Islamist terrorism is minimal compared with "ethno-nationalist" and "separatist" terrorism— terrorism committed by white people, in other words. According to Europol, in 2006, one out of 498 documented terrorist attacks across Europe could be classed as "Islamist"; in 2007, the figure rose to just four out of 583—that's less than 1 per cent of the total. By contrast, 517 attacks across the continent were claimed by or attributed to nationalist or separatist terrorist groups, such as ETA [Euskadi Ta Askatasuna] in Spain.

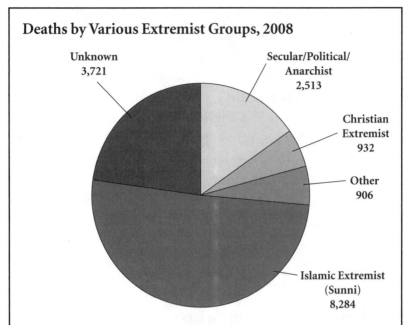

Deaths by Various Extremist Groups, 2008

Unknown
3,721

Secular/Political/
Anarchist
2,513

Christian
Extremist
932

Other
906

Islamic Extremist
(Sunni)
8,284

This chart represents 15,765 total deaths. There may be some double counting when joint claims were made. Categories include attacks either claimed, suspected, or inferred.

TAKEN FROM: National Counterterrorism Center, 2008 Report on Terrorism. www.nctc.gov.

It is not only liberals and aggrieved Muslims who are concerned about the under-reporting of white terrorism. One senior minister told me recently that he wished the British media would give greater coverage to non-Muslims on trial for terrorism and terror-related offences.

"It would help us a great deal with the Muslim community," the minister said. "It would show them that we prosecute violent extremists of all types—because they're all nasty bastards, be they Islamists or white supremacists."

Yet this, too, is slightly disingenuous. Compared to Islamists, who have been subjected to a battery of punitive measures—from detention without charge to control orders to torture abroad—white supremacists seem to be given preferential treatment by our criminal justice system. Robert Cottage was charged under the Explosive Substances Act 1883, not the panoply of modern anti-terror laws now at the disposal of the police and the Crown Prosecution Service. Neil MacGregor was tried in a sheriff's court, rather than the high court where such cases normally go, and where he would have faced a much more severe sentence. He was also tried on the ludicrously lenient charge of breaching the peace. It seems that in Britain, a white racist threatening to behead a Muslim a week is taken no more seriously than a man who is drunk and disorderly in public, or who keeps waking his neighbours with loud music.

Equal Treatment of Terrorists

Terrorists—those who deploy illegitimate violence against civilians for political purposes—should be ruthlessly identified, relentlessly pursued, arrested, prosecuted and punished, regardless of race or creed. Justice must be colour-blind, and seen to be colour-blind. Any other approach, by the authorities or the media, risks further alienating and stigmatising Muslim communities in Britain.

As we went to press, anti-terror detectives finally acknowledged that the door has been left open to potentially "spectacular" terror attacks of the far-right, white-supremacist variety—but I have yet to see this reported on any front page.

"There is a growing right-wing threat, not just al Qaeda," said Sir Norman Bettison, chief constable of West Yorkshire Police, in the wake of raids on a network of alleged far-right extremists in possession of 300 weapons and 80 bombs. It was the biggest seizure of suspected terrorist materials in England since the early 1990s, when the IRA [Irish Republican Army] was active.

Terrorism, we know, is not the exclusive preserve or franchise of dark-skinned, bearded Muslims. But nowadays you might not know it from following the news.

> "What makes the Christian Right who they are is their exclusive claim to being Christian and following Christian morality. In making this claim they also demonize anyone whose views challenge theirs."

The Christian Right Is Extremist

Jan G. Linn

Jan G. Linn is co-pastor of Spirit of Joy Christian Church in Lakeville, Minnesota, and author of several books that lobby for an inclusive, peacemaking view of Christianity. In the following viewpoint, written during the time when George W. Bush was president, Linn uses Bush as an example of a person with political power who belongs to the Christian Right. Linn contends that members of the Christian Right are extremist because they behave as if they alone know and do the will of God, particularly in political situations.

As you read, consider the following questions:

1. Linn says he sees nothing wrong with Mr. Bush claiming to be "born again." To what does he object?

2. What does Linn say is implied when the most powerful man in the world says he is being led by God to his actions?

3. How does Linn say non-Christians develop opinions about Christians? Does he think this is an accurate depiction?

Mr. [George W.] Bush has made public statements that leave little doubt about how he views his own job [president of the United States] and the role America must play in the world. In a conversation with Palestinian Prime Minister Mahmoud Abbas, he said,

> God told me to strike at al Qaeda and I struck them, and then he instructed me to strike at Saddam [Hussein], which I did, and now I am determined to solve the problem in the Middle East. If you help me, I will act, and if not, the elections will come and I will have to focus on them.

We see nothing wrong with Mr. Bush or any other political leader claiming to be a "born again" Christian, though we do admit it makes us very nervous when he claims his actions are based on God telling him what to do. Most troubling, however, is the fact that the Christian Right claims him as one of their own, and he seems to welcome it. In his book, *Persecution: How Liberals Are Waging War Against Christianity*, about which we will have much more to say later, David Limbaugh characterizes criticism of Bush and his policies as an attack on Bush's attempt to put his faith in action. In an extended section defending him, Limbaugh concludes,

> Christians cannot and should not build a firewall between their private lives and their public persona, between their Christianity and their governance. It is impossible for anyone, including the president, to separate his belief system, his worldview, from his public life.

His statement suggests that Mr. Bush is simply living out his faith. That is too simplistic. When the most powerful man in the world says he is being led by God to do what he does, it is much more than saying he is trying to live his faith. He is implying that to disagree with his decisions is to disagree with God. Moreover, what Limbaugh and the Christian Right ignore is the fact that Muslim terrorists whom they believe are the epitome of evil also claim to be serving God. Excessive radicalism can cut many ways. That one is a Christian does not justify political policies. Fundamentalist theology exists in Judaism and Islam as well as Christianity.

The Christian Right Labels Any Opposition as Immoral and Anti-Christian

This is not to say that all fundamentalists are members of the Christian Right. Many are not. Moreover, some of them, especially within academic institutions, have views that reflect both humility and open-mindedness, neither of which the Christian Right can be accused of demonstrating. More to the point, what distinguishes the Christian Right from other Christian fundamentalists is that its members *immerse their ultraconservative political views and agenda in Christian baptism*. They do not hesitate labeling anyone who disagrees with them as immoral and anti-Christian. This is done openly and in subtle ways, and is present in and through all their words and actions. It, in fact, drives them. They thrive on having an enemy who must be vanquished.

This is what sets the Christian Right apart. Political activism by Christians is not a new or bad thing. What makes the Christian Right who they are is their exclusive claim to being Christian and following Christian morality. In making this claim they also demonize anyone whose views challenge theirs. In their world, disagreement makes for enemies. Liberals are particularly that enemy. They are the people the Christian Right loves to hate. And that is not too strong a word to use when talking about the Christian Right. They speak of "hating the sin but loving the sinner," but fail miserably in their effort, if in fact they make any effort at all. They believe they are right because they are Christian and, therefore, have a corner on truth that is available to no one else. They hide their prejudice and close-mindedness behind a thin veil of religious slogans and Bible quotes that tell everything about them but nothing about the truth they claim to be espousing.

The Need for Debate on Human Terms

It's not that those who disagree with the Christian Right are always right on issues. What distinguishes us is that we do not believe God is on *our* side in our disagreements, or that *we alone* know the mind of God when it comes to complex issues. We do not call our opponents "godless" conservatives. We do not believe God is going to send them to "hell." We are willing, instead, to keep the debate on a human level and leave God out of it. We think that over the centuries Christians have done enough damage naming the enemies of God without our adding to it.

The Christian Right, of course, will have none of this. They are determined to drag God and the Bible into every comment they make about their enemies. We believe they are doing great damage to the nation and to Christianity. Non-Christians do not make the kinds of distinctions between Christians that we make among ourselves. Instead, they judge us by our public face, much the way Christians draw conclusions about other faith traditions. It distresses us that what non-Christians think of all Christians is in large part determined by what they hear from Christianity's loudest voice today, the Christian Right. But even more sobering is the danger the Christian Right poses to the enduring principles of this nation. They are convinced this is a Christian nation and are, therefore, working hard to transform our present form of government into a Christian state. We will show that to achieve

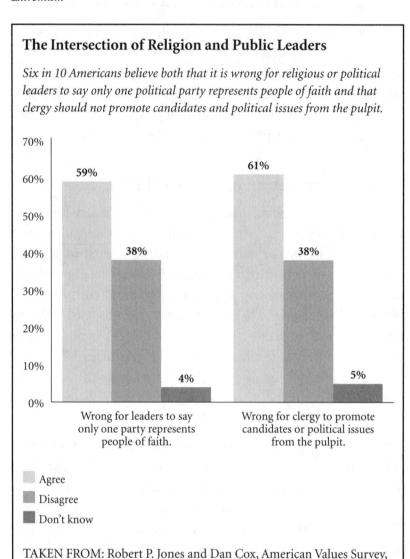

The Intersection of Religion and Public Leaders

Six in 10 Americans believe both that it is wrong for religious or political leaders to say only one political party represents people of faith and that clergy should not promote candidates and political issues from the pulpit.

Wrong for leaders to say only one party represents people of faith.
- Agree: 59%
- Disagree: 38%
- Don't know: 4%

Wrong for clergy to promote candidates or political issues from the pulpit.
- Agree: 61%
- Disagree: 38%
- Don't know: 5%

Agree
Disagree
Don't know

TAKEN FROM: Robert P. Jones and Dan Cox, American Values Survey, October 25, 2006. www.centerforamericanvalues.org.

this goal they have adopted an ethic of "ends justifying means." It is very troubling that a group of people who claim to be the only genuine Christians, and also the only true people of God, act this way. At the very least it requires those of us who claim to be of the same faith tradition to challenge what the Christian Right stands for and what it seeks to do.

Given who they are, it is little wonder they scare non-Christians. Truth be told, they scare other Christians! But not enough to keep us quiet.

> *"Until Tony Perkins or Jim Dobson puts a pistol on the table and threatens to kill someone, they shouldn't be called ayatollah of the Right or the jihadists of the Right."*

The Christian Right Is Not Extremist

Sarah Pulliam

In this viewpoint, Christianity Today's online editor Sarah Pulliam discusses the term "Religious Right," as well as related phrases such as "American Taliban" and "Christian fascists." She cites a number of prominent Christians who see these as pejorative terms, which they believe unfairly associate conservative Christians with extremist terrorists. They prefer to be described by other terms, such as "socially conservative evangelicals," which do not carry the same connotations of violence and terrorism.

As you read, consider the following questions:

1. How does Pulliam say the term "Religious Right" originated?

2. What does Jim Wallis, founder of *Sojourners*, say about the term "Religious Right"?

Sarah Pulliam, "Phrase 'Religious Right' Misused, Conservatives Say," *Christianity Today*, February 12, 2009. Copyright © 2009 Christianity Today. Reproduced by permission of the author.

3. Why does Family Research Council leader Tony Perkins want a different term?

The term "Religious Right" pops up every election cycle, but leaders often identified with the political movement say that while their constituencies remain strong, the catchphrase deserves a proper burial.

After election day, the BBC declared that times are uncertain for the Religious Right. In September 2008, *Newsweek* declared a Religious-Right Revival after Sarah Palin was nominated vice president. Even after the election, the term "Religious Right" or "Christian Right" appeared in recent obituaries as journalists searched for words to describe Paul Weyrich, cofounder of the Moral Majority, and the Rev. Richard John Neuhaus, founder of Catholic journal *First Things*.

However, several politically conservative evangelicals said in interviews that they do not want to be identified with the "Religious Right," "Christian Right," "Moral Majority," or other phrases still thrown around in journalism and academia.

"There is an ongoing battle for the vocabulary of our debate," said Gary Bauer, president of American Values. "It amazes me how often in public discourse really pejorative phrases are used, like the 'American Taliban,' 'fundamentalists,' 'Christian fascists,' and 'extreme Religious Right.'"

Jerry Falwell, cofounder of the Moral Majority, self-applied the Religious Right label until it started taking a more negative connotation, according to John Green, senior fellow at the Pew Forum on Religion & Public Life.

"Terminology is fraught with peril," Green said. "People associated it with hard-edge politics and intolerance. Very few people to whom that term now would apply would use that term."

Academics believe the phrase originated with the media in the late 1970s after politically conservative groups like the Moral Majority and the Christian Coalition were formed.

"I think some of these terms have a life of their own. There's very little you can do to change them and reinvent them," said Joel Carpenter, former Calvin College provost and author of *Revive Us Again: The Reawakening of American Fundamentalism.* "The Moral Majority no longer exists, but conservative religious folk who are pushing conservative cultural politics are still around."

Gary Schneeberger, vice president of media and public relations for Focus on the Family, said that when writers include terms like "Religious Right" and "fundamentalist," they can create negative impressions.

"Terms like 'Religious Right' have been traditionally used in a pejorative way to suggest extremism," Schneeberger said. "The phrase 'socially conservative evangelicals' is not very exciting, but that's certainly the way to do it."

What muddies the waters even more is when writers use the terms "evangelical" and "Religious Right" interchangeably. Individuals like megachurch pastor Rick Warren would resist being categorized as part of the Religious Right, even though the policies he supports may be politically conservative, said Randall Balmer, author of the *Encyclopedia of Evangelicalism.*

"I don't know if there are any labels for these folk," he said. "They do defy political labeling."

Like Warren, many groups would rather distance themselves from the Religious Right, even though they may agree on several political issues. Richard Land said he corrects numerous reporters who call him a leader of the Religious Right, explaining that he represents a group of Southern Baptists who would probably consider themselves conservative evangelicals.

"When the so-called 'Religious Right' agrees with us, we applaud their good taste and good judgment," said Land, who is president of the Ethics & Religious Liberty Commission of the Southern Baptist Convention. Some phrases need to be eliminated from journalists' vocabulary entirely, he said. "Until

Tony Perkins or Jim Dobson puts a pistol on the table and threatens to kill someone, they shouldn't be called ayatollah of the Right or the jihadists of the Right."

On the other side of the political spectrum, founder of *Sojourners* Jim Wallis is often associated with the "Religious Left" but would rather be called a progressive. He also dislikes the use of "Religious Right."

"I would not be happy with labeling anyone just right-wing. That's simplistic and reductionist," Wallis said. "Labels are shorthand, sloppy ways to describe someone."

Organizational leaders like Tony Perkins of Family Research Council want a term that includes other religious groups like Catholics, Jews, and Mormons so that they can see themselves as fighting for the same cause.

"It's not accurate to say that the Christian Right or the Religious Right is simply a narrow slice of evangelicals," Perkins said. "Will everyone identify themselves as part of the Religious Right? No, but they do share a portion of values."

Coming up with the best term to describe religious groups who are politically conservative can be tricky for writers. Rice University sociologist Bill Martin, who authored the book *With God on Our Side: The Rise of the Religious Right in America*, resists the term "religious conservative" because it has connotations with a group that identifies itself as theologically conservative.

"Mennonites and Amish are religious conservatives," Martin said. "They are pietistic people, but they're not involved politically."

Some journalists have already written obituaries for the Religious Right, but that would be premature, says Michael Cromartie, vice president at the Ethics and Public Policy Center.

"I think it's unwise to say any of these groups are finished," Cromartie said. "Groups like these often grow, regroup,

[or] expand when they're in opposition." In other words, perhaps journalists should find a style before 2012.

Editor's Note: See also *Christianity Today's* September 1999 cover story, "Is the Religious Right Finished?" More politics coverage is available at our politics blog and politics & law section.

Periodical Bibliography

The following articles have been selected to supplement the diverse views presented in this chapter.

Vanessa Baird	"In the Name of God: Are Violence and Religion Natural Bedfellows?" *New Internationalist*, August 1, 2004.
Catholic New Times	"A Conversation Between Joan Chittister and Bill Moyers: Benedictine Nun Joan Chittister Anguishes over American 'Moral Values,'" December 19, 2004.
Christian Century	"On the Left and Right, Activists Are Driven by Religious Convictions," October 20, 2009.
Frederick Clarkson	"History Is Powerful," *Public Eye Magazine*, Spring 2007.
John L. Esposito and Dalia Mogahed	"Battle for Muslims' Hearts and Minds: The Road Not (Yet) Taken," *Middle East Policy*, March 22, 2007.
Daniel Malotky	"Fundamentalist Violence and Despair," *Political Theology*, March 2009.
George Michael	"Strange Bedfellows," *Chronicle of Higher Education*, April 21, 2006.
Kenneth Minogue	"Fundamentalism Isn't the Problem," *New Criterion*, June 2004.
Mansoor Moaddel and Stuart A. Karabenick	"Religious Fundamentalism Among Young Muslims in Egypt and Saudi Arabia," *Social Forces*, June 2008.
Newsweek International	"Islamic Reaffirmation: Young Muslims Need to Learn That a Small Minority of Extremists Is Trying to Hijack Our Faith. So, Too, Do Opinion Makers in the West," November 28, 2005.

CHAPTER 2

What Motivates
Islamic Extremists?

Chapter Preface

There are millions of Muslims in the world. Yet only a small percentage of them can be considered extremists or terrorists. Several different perspectives explain this trend. Zeyno Baran of the Hudson Institute, in a 2008 testimony before the United States Senate Committee on Homeland Security and Governmental Affairs, describes one way of explaining the difference:

> The starting point has to be distinguishing between Muslims and Islamists, and between Islam (the religion) and Islamism (the political ideology). Islam, the religion, deals with piety, ethics, and beliefs, and can be compatible with secular liberal democracy and basic civil liberties. Islamists, however, believe Islam is the *only* basis for the legal and political system that governs the world's economic, social, and judicial mechanisms. Islamic law, or *sharia*, must shape all aspects of human society, from politics and education to history, science, the arts, and more. It is diametrically opposed to liberal democracy.

Baran continues by describing the way he sees new potential Islamists being recruited and then groomed to participate in violent acts. According to Baran, Islamist recruiters gain new members by first befriending them, then convincing them that political activism is necessary to defend Islam. Many are persuaded to take further steps, resulting in their willingness to participate in local, and then global, violence in the name of Islam. He emphasizes that the religious and ideological aspects are a part of this indoctrination process but that the social aspects, such as feeling like part of a community, are equally important motivators for committing violent acts.

Baran's theory, which first differentiates between *Islam* and *Islamism* and then points out a number of factors that can contribute to Islamism, illustrates the complexity of this issue.

The assumption cannot be made that someone who believes in Islam is necessarily an Islamist. Many Muslims and Islamic organizations throughout the world disagree with Islamists. They believe that violent acts of the Islamists are in direct conflict with their Muslim faith. For example, an online petition titled "Not in the Name of Islam," launched in 2004 by the Council on American-Islamic Relations, states,

> We, the undersigned Muslims, wish to state clearly that those who commit acts of terror, murder and cruelty in the name of Islam are not only destroying innocent lives, but are also betraying the values of the faith they claim to represent. No injustice done to Muslims can ever justify the massacre of innocent people, and no act of terror will ever serve the cause of Islam.

By 2006, more than seven hundred thousand individual Muslims and Muslim organizations had signed the petition.

The contrasting perspectives of Islamists and other Muslims show that it is not sufficient to point to only one underlying factor behind Islamic extremist terrorism, but rather it is necessary to look at a combination of causes. The following viewpoints examine some of the possible motivations behind extreme and violent acts committed by Islamists, with particular emphasis on how the religion of Islam contributes to these extremist actions.

| "One does not normally come to believe it is God's will for you to murder innocent strangers because you grew up poor, or hungry, or uneducated, or generally disadvantaged."

Islamic Extremists Are Motivated by Moral Disgust

Azeem Ibrahim

On Christmas Day 2009, a Nigerian Muslim man attempted to blow up a plane on its way to Detroit, Michigan, but was stopped by fellow passengers. In the following viewpoint, scholar and entrepreneur Azeem Ibrahim uses that incident to illustrate his belief that Islamic terrorists are motivated by moral disgust with Muslim suffering, rather than by poverty or lack of education, as some others believe. He describes the steps the Solas Foundation, a Scottish organization with which he is affiliated, takes to counter terrorism through education.

As you read, consider the following questions:

1. Briefly list former CIA officer Marc Sageman's four stages of Muslim radicalization, as described by Ibrahim.

Azeem Ibrahim, "Tackling the Real Causes of Islamic Extremism," *The Scotsman*, January 6, 2010. Copyright © 2010 Johnston Publishing Ltd. Reproduced by permission.

2. What does Ibrahim believe is the one way to beat terrorism?

3. Name three things that the Solas Foundation does to beat terrorism.

The events surrounding the terrorist attempt on Christmas Day [2009] are becoming common knowledge: how the 23-year-old alleged bomber [Umar Farouk Abdulmutallab] was the son of a wealthy Nigerian financier who warned United States diplomats that his son might be a security risk; how the young man had studied mechanical engineering at University College London and lived in a luxury apartment; how he dropped out of a postgraduate business course in Dubai to travel to Yemen; how he apparently got past airport security with 80g of highly explosive, colourless PETN crystals hidden in his trousers; how a heroic passenger jumped on him when he saw fire coming from his seat, and a larger group of fellow passengers held him down.

But in the days since the incident, one of the questions I have heard most frequently has been some variant on: "How could a young man in his position want to do it?" "How, with such a good education? How, coming from such a well-off family? How, given all the chances in life? How, when he had every opportunity to make so much of himself?"

These are natural questions to ask. But they are based on an incorrect premise and a fundamental misunderstanding of what drives young men to become radicals.

All these questions assume that there is some link between disadvantage and radicalisation. In fact, the evidence is that there is not. One does not normally come to believe it is God's will for you to murder innocent strangers because you grew up poor, or hungry, or uneducated, or generally disadvantaged. So those who wonder why a young man with such advantages could want to be a terrorist are barking up the wrong tree.

To understand why young men turn to terrorism, we need evidence.

Former CIA [Central Intelligence Agency] case officer Marc Sageman has made one of the most thorough analyses of al Qaeda networks ever conducted. He assembled more than 500 profiles of individual terrorists, their personal characteristics and motivations, how they were recruited and how they are organised.

Terrorists Are Motivated by Moral Disgust

What he discovers is that terrorists are most likely to be motivated not by disadvantage but by a sense of moral disgust.

He sets out four stages by which this radicalisation normally happens.

It is sparked when the individual reacts to stories of Muslim suffering around the world with moral outrage. Some of those who feel outraged will progress to the second stage, in which they interpret that suffering in the context of a wider Manichaean war between Islam and the West.

Of those who take that view, a minority will progress to the third stage, in which their smouldering resentment will be fuelled by bad personal experiences in Western countries, such as discrimination, inequality or just an inability to get on despite good qualifications.

Of those who undergo these three stages, fewer undergo the fourth, in which the individual joins a circle of friends which becomes like a family closed to the outside world, which shuts out the critical thinking which might challenge the radical worldview. They read, listen to and watch only material which stokes their view of the world and prepares them for action and, in some cases, the murder of innocents.

Terrorism Must Be Understood to Be Defeated

Why does all this matter? It matters because we cannot beat the radicalisation which leads to terrorism unless we first understand it.

I believe, and have argued publicly, that there is only one way to beat terrorism over the long term: reduce the motivation for young people to radicalise in the first place. It is no good trying only to dismantle terrorist networks. As the Christmas Day attack shows, a determined terrorist does not need a group to stage an attack—they just need the kind of know-how they can access online. It should not be a surprise that US homeland security secretary Janet Napolitano has said that there was no indication that this alleged attacker was "part of anything larger".

The Solas Foundation in Scotland is showing one way that we can break the link between perceptions of foreign policy and radicalisation, and provide the kind of education in authentic Islamic scholarship which delegitimises the violent methods of Islamic extremists. I believe that this is the best way to reduce the motivation to radicalise.

Terrorism Can Be Prevented by Changing Minds

What we are aiming for is not cure but prevention, the quiet changing of minds that cuts off the attraction of radical discourses at the root. We set Islamic teachings in their proper context. We give advice on how to apply Muslim ethics in modern society to both Islamic organisations and non-Islamic organisations who would like to tailor their services better to Muslims. And we work to educate a new generation of community leaders, educators and advocates who will be able to strengthen the British Muslim community. Crucially, the Solas Foundation is run by teachers who are credible to young people. Both of our leading scholars, Shaykh Amer Jamil and

Shaykh Ruzwan Mohammed, were born and educated in the West, before travelling and studying in the Muslim world with some of the leading Islamic theologians.

This combination of width of both scholarship and personal experience makes them uniquely qualified to relate to young people, teach Islamic scholarship authoritatively and explain how it fits into a modern context.

They are also prime examples of how Solas will encourage homegrown scholars, so that, in time, British mosques can reduce their reliance on preachers from abroad, who often cannot relate to the issues of the day.

Ultimately, the Solas Foundation will be a success if young people no longer interpret the news they see on TV with reference to extreme and narrow perversions of the rich traditions of Islam. Because, as the privileged biography of the Christmas Day attacker showed, it was the disgust that that news provoked which provokes radicalisation, not disadvantage.

We misunderstand the causes of this kind of terrorism at our peril.

"Terrorism spreads, in part, through
bad ideas. The most dangerous and seductive bad idea spreading around the
globe today is a distorted and destructive interpretation of Islam, which asserts that killing innocents is a way to
worship God."

Islamic Extremists Are Motivated by Social and Psychological Needs

Jessica Stern

*Jessica Stern is a lecturer at Harvard Law School. She has been
involved with several programs designed to deradicalize terrorists
in locations including the Netherlands, Iraq, and Saudi Arabia.
In the following viewpoint, she describes a number of social and
psychological factors she believes contribute to the radicalization
of terrorists, including religious ideology, social grievances, group
dynamics, and economics.*

Jessica Stern, "Mind over Martyr: How to Deradicalize Islamic Extremists," *Foreign
Affairs*, vol. 89, January–February 2010, p. 95. Copyright © 2010 by the Council
on Foreign Relations, Inc. Reproduced by permission of the publisher. www.foreign
affairs.org.

As you read, consider the following questions:

1. What does Stern say about the religious knowledge of people who claim to be driven by Islamic religious ideology?

2. Why does Stern say group dynamics sometimes attract young people to terrorist movements?

3. How does Stern say sexual abuse contributes to radicalization?

I first got involved in deradicalization efforts [of terrorists] in 2005, soon after the murder of the Dutch filmmaker Theo van Gogh by an Islamist militant. The city of Rotterdam recruited me to help develop a new concept of citizenship that would include Dutch natives as well as immigrants and their children; the city government worried that the idea of jihad [holy war] had become a fad among not only Muslim youth but also recent converts to Islam. In 2007, a company under contract with Task Force 134, the task force in charge of U.S.-run detention centers in Iraq, asked me to help develop a deradicalization program for the 26,000 Iraqis held at Camp Bucca and Camp Cropper (Camp Bucca has since been closed). Last winter [2008–09], together with a group of current and former U.S. government officials and analysts, I visited Riyadh's Care Rehabilitation Center, an institution that reintegrates convicted terrorists into Saudi society through religious reeducation, psychological counseling, and assistance finding a job. And in the spring of 2009, I visited a youth center supported by the Muslim Contact Unit, part of the Special Branch of the Metropolitan Police in London, which works with leaders of the Muslim community there, including Islamists, to isolate and counter supporters of terrorist violence.

These experiences made one thing clear: any rehabilitation effort must be based on a clear understanding of what drives people to terrorism in the first place. Terrorist movements often arise in reaction to an injustice, real or imagined, that they feel must be corrected. Yet ideology is rarely the only, or even the most important, factor in an individual's decision to join the cause. The reasons that people become terrorists are as varied as the reasons that others choose their professions: market conditions, social networks, education, individual preferences. Just as the passion for justice and law that drives a lawyer at first may not be what keeps him working at a law firm, a terrorist's motivations for remaining in, or leaving, his "job" change over time. Deradicalization programs need to take account—and advantage—of these variations and shifts in motivations.

Terrorists Are Often Ignorant About Islam

Interestingly, terrorists who claim to be driven by religious ideology are often ignorant about Islam. Our hosts in Riyadh told us that the vast majority of the deradicalization program's "beneficiaries," as its administrators call participants, had received little formal education and had only a limited understanding of Islam. In the Netherlands and elsewhere in Europe, second- and third-generation Muslim youth are rebelling against the kind of "soft" Islam practiced by their parents and promoted in local mosques. They favor what they think is the "purer" Islam, uncorrupted by Western culture, which is touted on some Web sites and by self-appointed imams [religious leaders] from the Middle East who are barely educated themselves. For example, the Netherlands-based terrorist cell known as the Hofstad Group designed what one police officer described as a "do-it-yourself" version of Islam based on interpretations of takfiri ideology (takfir is the practice of accusing other Muslims of apostasy) culled from the Internet and the teachings of a drug dealer turned cleric.

Such true believers are good candidates for the kind of ideological reeducation undertaken by Task Force 134 in Iraq and by the prison-based deradicalization program in Saudi Arabia. A Saudi official told the group of us who visited the

Care Rehabilitation Center in Riyadh last winter that the main reason for terrorism was ignorance about the true nature of Islam. Clerics at the center teach that only the legitimate rulers of Islamic states, not individuals such as Osama bin Laden, can declare a holy war. They preach against takfir and the selective reading of religious texts to justify violence. One participant in the program told us, "Now I understand that I cannot make decisions by reading a single verse. I have to read the whole chapter."

Prejudice Against Muslims Encourages Terrorism

In Europe, Muslim youth describe themselves, often accurately, as victims of prejudice in the workplace and in society more generally. Surveys carried out in 2006 by the European Monitoring Centre on Racism and Xenophobia (now subsumed by the Fundamental Rights Agency), an EU [European Union] body, showed that minorities and immigrants in the European Union experience greater levels of unemployment, are overrepresented in the least desirable jobs, and receive lower wages. After the van Gogh murder, the native Dutch, who are famously proud of their tolerance, grew visibly less so: They started complaining about rising rates of criminality among Dutch Moroccan youth and the rhetoric of radical imams who preach that homosexuality is a sickness or a sin. Rightly perceiving that this growing prejudice against Muslims could become a source of social conflict, local governments and nongovernmental organizations put in place various programs to integrate young immigrants into broader Dutch society.

Group dynamics are as important as social grievances. Young people are sometimes attracted to terrorist movements through social connections, music, fashion, or lifestyle and only later come to understand fully the groups' violent ideologies and goals. Al-Shabab, spurred by a member who calls himself Abu Mansour Al-Amriki, and other groups affiliated with al Qaeda have begun using anti-American hip-hop—"jihad rap"—in their recruitment videos; the British rap group Blakstone and the defunct but still popular American band Soldiers of Allah promote violence against *kafir* (nonbelievers). The first- and second-generation Muslim children I interviewed for a study of the sources of radicalization in the Netherlands seemed to think that talking about jihad was cool, in the same way that listening to gangster rap is in some youth circles. Most of these children will not turn to violence, but once youth join an extremist group, the group itself can become an essential part of their identity, maybe even their only community. And so deradicalization requires finding new sources of social support for them. The Saudi program takes great pains to reintegrate participants into their families and the communities they belonged to before their radicalization by encouraging family visits and getting the community involved in their follow-up after they are released. The program rightly assumes that group dynamics are key to both radicalization and deradicalization.

Then there is economics. For some, jihad is just a job. According to studies by the economist Alan Krueger, now the U.S. Treasury Department's assistant secretary for economic policy, and Alberto Abadie, a professor of public policy at Harvard, there is no direct correlation between low GDP [gross domestic product] and terrorism. Nonetheless, poor people in countries with high levels of unemployment are more vulnerable to recruitment. Of the 25,000 insurgents and terrorist suspects detained in Iraq as of 2007, nearly all were previously underemployed and 78 percent were unemployed, according to Major General Douglas Stone, the commander of Task Force 134 at the time. Because these insurgents took up the "job" of fighting a military occupation, typically targeting soldiers rather than civilians, at least some of them could conceivably be rehabilitated once foreign troops leave Iraq. According to Christopher Boucek, an expert on Saudi Arabia and Yemen at the Carnegie Endowment for International Peace, the advisory committee, which helps run the deradicalization program in Saudi Arabia, has reported that most detainees are men in their 20s from large lower- or middle-class families; only three percent come from high-income backgrounds. Boucek says that according to Saudi officials, 25 percent of the detained terrorists who had participated in jihad had prior criminal records, approximately half of them for drug-related offenses; only five percent were prayer leaders or had other formal religious roles. For such individuals, job training and career counseling may be the best deradicalization strategy—or at least a strategy as important as religious reeducation.

Rebuilding Self-Esteem Can Help Fight Terrorism

Psychology also matters. One element worth examining in particular is the potential impact of sexual abuse on radicalization. Much has been written about the role of radical madrasahs [traditional Islamic schools] in creating terrorists in Pakistan and elsewhere, some of it in these pages. Outside of the Pakistani press, however, little note is made of the routine rape of boys at such schools. Also troubling is the rape of boys by warlords, the Afghan National Army, or the police in Afghanistan. Such abuses are commonplace on Thursdays, also known as "man-loving day," because Friday prayers are considered to absolve sinners of all wrongdoing. David Whetham, a specialist in military ethics at King's College London, reports that security checkpoints set up by the Afghan police and military have been used by some personnel to troll for attractive young men and boys on Thursday nights. The local population has been forced to accept these episodes as par for the course: They cannot imagine defying the all-powerful Afghan commanders. Could such sexual traumas be

Social Conditions Cause Terrorism

What we should really be focusing on is not the decision of this or that individual (particularly not leaders such as [Osama] bin Laden, who are highly atypical even in their own movements) to become a terrorist. Rather, we should be looking at the social conditions that make dissident movements more likely to turn to terror and—more importantly—the circumstances under which such dissident movements receive popular support. Such an approach may also provide us with invaluable keys with which to distinguish between the limited success of a terrorist like Timothy McVeigh [the Oklahoma City bomber who killed 168 people in 1995]—who was met with no popular support—and the broad backing that Osama bin Laden and al Qaeda enjoy. When thinking about terrorism, we have to remind ourselves that it is primarily within a troubled and desperate social, economic, and cultural environment that the engineers of terrorism can freely recruit and operate, thus causing greater dangers to global society.

Ömer Taşpinar, *"Fighting Radicalism, Not 'Terrorism':*
Root Causes of an International Actor Redefined,"
SAIS Review, *Summer–Fall 2009, p. 83.*

a form of humiliation that contributes to contemporary Islamist terrorism? Similarly, one need not spend many days in Gaza before understanding that fear and humiliation, constants of daily life there, play at least some role in certain Palestinians' decisions to become martyr-murderers. If terrorism can be a source of validation, then surely helping adherents come to terms with the humiliation they have experienced could help bring them back into the fold. To that end, the Saudi rehabilitation program includes classes in self-esteem.

Aside from the question of preexisting personal trauma, consider the impact of a terrorist's lifestyle on his psychology. Exposure to violence, especially for those who become fighters, can cause lasting, haunting changes in the body and the mind. Terrorists are "at war," at least from their perspective, and they, too, may be at risk of post-traumatic stress disorder. Moreover, those who have been detained may have been subjected to torture and left with even more serious psychological wounds. The Guantánamo [Bay, a U.S. detainment facility in Cuba] detainees sent back to Saudi Arabia have posed a particular problem for the Saudi government, for example. One graduate of the facility in Riyadh told me privately that although he was taking psychotropic medications, which helped, he was still suffering from terrible nightmares and feeling hypervigilant. (He claimed to have been tortured with electrodes in Afghanistan, prior to being moved to Guantánamo.) It will be critically important to incorporate some of what the medical community learns about post-traumatic stress disorder. This is not because terrorists deserve sympathy—they do not—but because understanding their state of mind is necessary to limiting the risk that they will return to violence. . . .

Terrorism Spreads Through Bad Ideas

Terrorism continues to pose a significant threat to civilians around the world. If every terrorist could be killed or captured and then kept locked up indefinitely, the world would be a safer place. But there are limitations to this approach. Often, the only evidence implicating captured terrorists is not usable in court, and some terrorists will inevitably be released if they are returned to their countries of origin. The destructive ideology that animates the al Qaeda movement is spreading around the globe, including, in some cases, to small-town

America. Homegrown zealots, motivated by al Qaeda's distorted interpretation of Islam, may not yet be capable of carrying out 9/11-style strikes [like the airplane crashes on September 11, 2001], but they could nonetheless terrorize a nation.

Terrorism spreads, in part, through bad ideas. The most dangerous and seductive bad idea spreading around the globe today is a distorted and destructive interpretation of Islam, which asserts that killing innocents is a way to worship God. Part of the solution must come from within Islam and from Islamic scholars, who can refute this ideology with arguments based on theology and ethics. But bad ideas are only part of the problem. Terrorists prey on vulnerable populations—people who feel humiliated and victimized or who find their identities by joining extremist movements. Governments' arsenals against terrorism must include tools to strengthen the resilience of vulnerable populations. These tools should look more like anti-gang programs and public diplomacy than war.

> "The qur'ânic promise is that if only the true Muslims will ... open fire on the unbelievers God himself will intervene on their behalf and change everything."

Islamic Jihad Requires Killing the Enemy

Bill Musk

Bill Musk is an Anglican bishop in Egypt and has written several books on Christianity and Islam. In the following viewpoint, taken from his book The Certainty Trap: Can Christians and Muslims Afford the Luxury of Fundamentalism?, *Musk discusses Islamist (fundamentalist Islamic) beliefs that the holy struggle known as* jihad *requires physical fighting against enemies to achieve an Islamic state.*

As you read, consider the following questions:

1. What does the Muslim Brotherhood slogan, quoted by Musk, say is the highest hope?
2. What is a *fatwa*? Give an example.

Bill Musk, *The Certainty Trap: Can Christians and Muslims Afford the Luxury of Fundamentalism?* Pasadena, CA: William Carey Library, 2008. Copyright © 2008 by Bill A. Musk. Reproduced by permission. The reprinted material has been excerpted from the original chapter.

3. How does Faraj criticize those Muslims who withdraw from society, according to Musk?

American, Russian, Spanish—and more recently British—minds have had to try and wrestle with the reality that some peoples' interpretation of a holy text leads them to terrorise others in unthinkable ways. Innocent civilians, including women and children—people of all faiths and none—are randomly targeted by suicidal hit-squads composed of young adult Muslims. The men forming those hit-squads evidently believe that they are doing what God is ordering them to do. Their actions are accompanied by spiritual preparation and initiated with prayer. The cry upon their lips as they die is "Allahu akbar!" or "God is great!" Their reward for killing the "unbelievers" will be to gain quick access to paradise, plus they will accrue honour as "martyrs" for the Islamic cause. How can Westerners of any variety ever come to appreciate that sort of mind-set in the world of the twenty-first century?

If Westerners find the issue of Islamist terrorism an unnerving challenge to their understanding of what life might be about, a greater challenge, it seems to me, is the one that is put before contemporary *Muslims* by their fellow-Muslim extremists. How can today's orthodox Muslim community *not* appreciate the mind-set of the Islamists? After all, it claims to derive from the Qur'ân. It claims to be based on the example of Prophet Muhammad. It purports to have the support of famous Islamic theologians. It is evidently actioned by contemporary religious spokesmen—people knowing well the data of revelation—who give their consent or approval to violent forms of "holy war".

Finding Jihad in the Holy Text

In other words, the actions and beliefs of contemporary Islamists constitute, I am convinced, the greatest challenge to the traditional hermeneutic of certainty within Islam. Why?

Because those Islamists are saying: "Listen! Ours is the original, most faithful interpretation of the Qur'ân! Our interpretation is consistent with how Prophet Muhammad himself lived out his 'submission' to God! We are the true Muslims here!"

The Islamists are nitpickers about holy text and are fired with an ideological vision. They repeatedly quote chapter and verse of the Qur'ân in order to justify their beliefs and actions.

What they are waging is *holy* war—that is the point. It is fighting that originates in the will of God. *Jihâd* comprises part of Muslim faithfulness in submission to God's will.

In order to appreciate where such Islamists are coming from, we need to recognise the importance within Islam of the concept of *ijtihâd*. The Arabic word literally means "exertion" and refers to a deduction on a legal or theological matter that is made by a *mujtahid* or knowledgeable theologian. How to work out what it means to be a Muslim in the world is the task of a *mujtahid*. The spectrum of opinion represented by the proponents of *ijtihâd* may range from the most liberal to the ultraconservative. . . .

Jihad Justifies the Use of Force

During the twentieth century, emerging initially as part of the general Muslim move towards finding a theological rationale for opposing dominating imperial powers, a renewed Islamist genre of *ijtihâd* developed alongside other Muslim perspectives. People in the tradition of Sayyid Abû'l-'Alâ' Mawdûdî and Sayyid Qutb came to produce theological perspectives that justified the use of force in fulfillment of a scriptural requirement for *jihâd*. The well-known slogan of the Muslim Brotherhood well expresses their motivation and priorities:

Allah is our objective.

The Messenger is our leader.

The Qur'ân is our law.

> *Jihâd* is our way.
> Dying in the way of Allah is our
> highest hope.

Ijtihâd, then, provides the permission and precedent for Islamists contemporary reinterpreting of Islam's holy text. Often, as a result of such re-interpretative "exertion", a *fatwâ* or legal opinion comes to be made—declaring that it is right in God's eyes, for example, to target foreign tourists in Luxor and Sharm al-Sheikh, or to "kill Americans everywhere," or to capture schoolchildren in Beslan, or to set a fiery cross ablaze in the heart of London's transportation system. The Islamists rely in their *ijtihâd* on the opinions of earlier, famous, radical theologians—people like Ibn Hanbal, founder of the conservative "Hanbalite" school of Islamic jurisprudence. They comprise a modern continuation of a radical and historical stream of qur'ânic interpretation within Islam. As such, they call into question previous and traditional understandings of what the Qur'ân says. Their pet subject, it would seem, is the concept of holy war or *jihâd*. What does *jihâd* really mean, they ask?

The Islamists' calling into question of traditional views (of *jihâd*, for example) must, surely, comprise a massive challenge to the supposed or assumed idea that the Qur'ân can only ever have one (historic) meaning. It wrong-foots those spokespersons for Islam who operate within a hermeneutic of certainty but who now find themselves accused of lacking certainty where, in the view of the Islamist, the Qur'ân gives such sureness. It makes it hard for most Muslims not to feel condemned for their own comparative lack of self-sacrificing commitment to the word given by God.

Jihad Is Considered the "Neglected Duty" of Islamists

Let me illustrate my "take" on the Islamists and scripture from the group involved in the assassination of President Anwar Sadat of Egypt in October 1981. My family was living in Egypt

Radical Islamists Believe Only Martyrs Are Guaranteed Salvation

Radicals believe the only true assurance or secure promise of eternal salvation for a Muslim is to be a martyr—and ideally a suicide bomber—in the cause of jihad.

"The call to Jihad in God's name," wrote Osama bin Laden and his colleagues in 1984 in the first issue of their recruiting magazine, *Jihad*, "leads to eternal life in the end, and is relief from your earthly chains."

"A martyr will not feel the pain of death except like how you feel when you are pinched," bin Laden told his followers in 1996 in his formal declaration of war against the United States. "A martyr's privileges are guaranteed by God; forgiveness with the first gush of his blood, he will be shown his seat in Paradise, he will be decorated with the jewels of [belief], married off to the beautiful ones ... assured security in the Day of Judgment ... [and] wedded to seventy-two of the pure [virgin women of Paradise]."

Bin Laden went on to assert that "without shedding of blood, no degradation and branding can be removed from the forehead."

Put another way, bin Laden both believes and preaches that if a Muslim sheds his blood and loses his life in the cause of jihad, then he will have all his bad deeds removed from the scales. What's more, he uses the concept of the assurance of salvation through martyrdom as a recruiting tool, offering hope to Muslims who fear hell more than death.

Joel C. Rosenberg, Inside the Revolution.
Carol Stream, IL: Tyndale, 2009.

during that period of Islamist anger with their national leader. Sadat's executioners were motivated by a relatively young ideologue, Muhammad 'Abd al-Salâm Faraj. This intelligent man was a graduate in electrical engineering from Cairo University. In the late 1970s, while working in Alexandria, he was recruited to the Egyptian Islamist group called *al-Jihâd*. When the leaders of that group's cell in Alexandria were arrested, the cell fizzled out. Faraj, however, avoided arrest because he was not one of the cell's leaders. At some point Faraj moved back to Cairo where he obtained employment at the University of Cairo. Over the next year or so, he worked clandestinely with a couple of other men to bring together various Islamist cells to form a new *al-Jihâd* group.

During the summer of 1980, Faraj authored a pamphlet that would eventually be refuted, point by point, by none less than the Mufti of Egypt. That refutation was printed in a national newspaper two months after Sadat's death. Faraj's pamphlet expresses the ideology behind the militancy of the men who saw Sadat as standing in the way of God's will for Egypt. As such, it illustrates the challenge that Islamism poses for orthodox Muslims concerning their view of the Qur'ân as comprising God's revelation to them.

The title of Faraj's work is *The Neglected Duty (Al-Farîda al-Ghâ'iba)*. It begins by quoting the Qur'ân:

> Has not the Time arrived for the Believers that their hearts in all humility should engage in the remembrance of Allah and of the Truth which has been revealed (to them), and that they should not become like those to whom was given Revelation aforetime, but long ages passed over them and their hearts grew hard? For many among them are rebellious transgressors. (Sura 57:16)

The "neglected duty" is, of course, *jihâd*. Faraj aims to stir his readership to an armed struggle against the rebellious transgressors in contemporary Egyptian society. Although President Sadat is never mentioned by name in the text of the pamphlet, it is obvious that his regime constitutes the current infidel or apostate state against which *jihâd* must be waged. Faraj's constant theme is that the contemporary "spiritual" health of Muslims in Egypt is far from what God would have it to be.

Those seeking to bring about a positive change in that state of health are going about it in the wrong way, claims Faraj in the opening section of his pamphlet. The benevolent societies, of which there are thousands in Egypt, may do a lot of good work in the short term but do they bring about the foundation of an Islamic state? The Sûfî movement may assist many Egyptian Muslims with growing in personal piety but by doing so they help too many Egyptians miss the wood for the trees: the common goal has to be, not more piety, but obedience to God's Word—bringing in the rule of God.

The Muslim Brotherhood (an avowedly Islamist group) and other reformists aim to achieve some change by getting involved in Egyptian politics and exerting pressure from within the party system. Faraj suggests that all political parties collaborate to some extent with the state within which they are active. Other radical Egyptian Muslims seek to proceed by infiltrating the government apparatus. Perhaps the author has in mind here Sheikh al-Sha'râwî, a popular religious leader with a strong TV following who climbed to being a Cabinet Minister in the late 1970s. An infiltrator, however, has still to show support of the status quo, and such support would naturally exclude him from being in a position to deny the status quo and inaugurate something totally different.

What about those fellow Islamists or reformists who withdraw from *jâhilî* society to form their own, faithful "groups of separation" that live apart from fellow Muslims, in caves or furnished apartments, in a "true" Islamic setting? Faraj's words here constitute a critical reference to fellow Islamists who took to withdrawing from Egyptian polity in the 1970s in order to live in communes within caves in the countryside or within furnished apartments on the edges of various cities. There they sought to live as "true" Muslims, away from a depraved or *jâhilî* society. Faraj asks how that kind of procedure can bring into reality an Islamic state.

An Islamic State Can Be Obtained Only by Jihad

Faraj looks round the contemporary Islamic scene in Egypt and declares that all existing routes to reform miss the essential method, authenticated by God himself and clearly declared within the Qur'ân. That method is *jihâd*. The only way to bring about an Islamic state is for a small minority of Muslims to become radically committed to *jihâd* in the sense of armed struggle. The qur'ânic promise is that if only the true Muslims will take the initiative and obey God's command to *jihâd*, then as they open fire on the unbelievers God himself will intervene on their behalf and change everything:

> Fight them, and Allah will punish them by your hands, cover them with shame, help you (to victory) over them, heal the breasts of Believers . . . (Sura 9:14)

The establishment of an Islamic state on earth is clearly God's intention. Therefore it is God who is responsible for working out the details of how that establishment comes about as the true Muslims begin to obey him by fighting for it. Faraj was promoting a faith project.

Faraj also deals in detail with military tactics, explaining the methodology for fighting as it is advocated in the Qur'ân and by prophetic example (in the *sunna* of the Prophet, recorded in the *hadîth* literature). After all, the faith-fighting has to be done in the prescribed manner in order for God to lend to it his authority. Authorised tactics include: the use of deception; the infiltrating of the ranks of the foe; the acceptability of killing women and children en route to routing the main enemy; and the allowance for destroying the material and natural heritage of the enemy. In other words, tactics of terror are specifically allowed or authorised by appeal to the records of what Prophet Muhammad said or did or approved. . . .

Fighting Is Obligatory

The end result of all the abrogation is that, quite clearly, fighting is made obligatory. Faraj's point is that "fighting" means fighting—*jihâd* means the sword. You cannot interpret these abrogating verses in any way other than in the sense of physical combat. His conclusion is simply and forcefully put. When God made the duty of fasting obligatory, he (God) announced: "Fasting is prescribed to you" (Sura 2:183). Similarly, with regard to the duty of *jihâd*, God declared: "Fighting is prescribed for you" (Sura 2:216). Thus, says Faraj, "the [real character of this] duty is clearly spelled out in the text of the Qur'ân: It is fighting, which means confrontation and blood".

> *"Osama bin Laden's statements are shrouded in religious references, but he cites the persecution of Islam in communal terms: 'Its sons are being killed, its blood is being shed, its holy places are being attacked.'"*

Suicide Bombers Are Motivated by Social Rather than Religious Injustice

Nichole Argo

Nichole Argo, a doctoral student in political science and international studies, spent several years living in the Middle East. In the following viewpoint, she contends that suicide bombers are not primarily motivated by religious ideals but by social relationships and as a reaction to perceived injustice.

As you read, consider the following questions:

1. Why does Argo use the term "human bombs" rather than "suicide bombers"?
2. According to Marc Sageman's study of the global Salafi jihad, how were most of the members drawn to be part of the network?

Nichole Argo, "Human Bombs: Rethinking Religion and Terror," MIT Center for International Studies Audit of the Conventional Wisdom, April 2006, pp. 1–4. Reproduced by permission of the author.

3. What reason does Argo give that makes normal individuals able to kill? What additional criteria lead them to make costly sacrifices to do so?

Suicide terror has become a daily news staple. Who are these human bombs, and why are they willing to die in order to kill? Many observers turn to Islam for an explanation. They cite the preponderance of Muslim bombers today, indoctrination by extremist institutions, and the language used in jihadi statements [promoting holy war].

But these arguments fall short. At present, bombers are primarily Muslim, but this was not always so. Nor does indoctrination play a strong role in growing today's self-selected global jihad networks. Rather, militants and bombers are propelled by social ties. And even when jihadis use the Qur'an and Sunna to frame their struggle, their justifications for violence are primarily secular and grievance-based.

So what is religion's role? Almost 100 years ago, [French sociologist] Émile Durkheim contended that religious ideation is born of sentiment. This is worth considering in the current context. Against the repression, alienation, and political helplessness of the Muslim world, jihad speaks of individual dignity and communal power. 'Against the Goliaths,' martrydom says, 'even one bursting body can make a difference.' The Muslim street is buying it, though sometimes ambivalently. To stop the bombers of today and tomorrow, we need to figure out why.

Suicide Bombers Are a Product of Several Factors

Suicide attacks have been a prominent tactic in insurgent movements since the 1970s. Then, analysts believed that bombers and their masterminds were irrational, if not crazy, or had given up on life because of desperate circumstances such as poverty, depression, or social failure. However, data that have since been compiled show that suicide attackers come not from the criminal, illiterate, or poor, but from largely secular and educated middle classes. They do not exhibit signs of sociopathy or depression, nor do they appear to have suffered more than their respective populations. Surprisingly, many are volunteers, rather than recruits. There is, in short, no individual-level profile for a suicide bomber. Human bombs are a product of structural, social, and individual interactions.

Rather than evince suicidal tendencies—as the term "suicide bombers" connotes—psychological autopsies of past and would-be bombers show many of these individuals to be wholly, even altruistically invested in life. As a result, it is more apt—and less misleading—to refer to these individuals as "human bombs" rather than "suicide bombers."

Religion Is Not the Primary Motivator for Suicide Bombers

Since 9/11 [September 11, 2001, terrorist attacks on the United States], the notion that terror is bound to religious extremism has almost become an implicit assumption. This is easy to understand. If bombers were once "normal" people, then religious indoctrination could explain their fanatical behavior. Moreover, the numbers are powerful: 81 percent of suicide attacks since 1968 have occurred after 2001, with 31 out of the 35 organizations responsible being jihadi. Even the London and Bali (II) bombers who acted independently of terror organizations were Muslim. It would be difficult to deny that Islamic inspiration is at work in the motivation and mobilization of rising terror. But how? Inspiration is not causation, and a growing body of data suggest that Islamic indoctrination and belief are not the answer. Below, I audit several arguments commonly offered in support of the religious terror thesis.

1. Muslims perpetrate most of today's terror, so most terror must be motivated by Islam. At present, 31 of 35 organizations perpetrating suicide terror are Muslim. But five years ago [in 2001], a majority of attacks were carried out by secular rather than religious organizations. Because religion-terror correlations have changed over time, they tell us little about causation. Even if the statistics were stable, it is not possible to infer bomber motivations from organizational charters. Rather than ask who is perpetrating the attacks, we need to ask why.

Here history can help. Martyr missions made their official twentieth-century debut in the Second World War with the Kamikazes; they showed up again in the 1960s, when Viet Cong sympathizers exploded themselves amidst U.S. troops. Their debut in the Islamic world was not until the 1980s, during the Iran-Iraq War. Facing a far superior Iraqi military, Ayatollah Khomeini rounded up children by the tens of thousands and sent them in "human waves" to overrun the enemy. While Persians accrued losses in the war against Iraq, the role of the martyr in defensive jihad was exalted. As in U.S. wars, the dead became heroes.

The Iranian example had seismic effects. Lebanese groups appropriated the notion of a martyr's death almost immediately, employing human bombs against Israeli and international presences in Lebanon as early as 1981. Half of the human bombs in Lebanon were perpetrated by secular organizations. The Tamil Tigers of Sri Lanka perfected the tactic, becoming the most professional cadre in the world. Human bombs were also used by the Kurdish PKK [the Workers' Party, a separatist organization] against Turkey, the Sikhs in India, and the Palestinians against Israel, to name a few.

When we think of suicide bombers, we think of extremism. But the cases above locate the bomber as one popularly supported element in a coherent campaign of resistance against a perceived occupier, and such was true for 95 percent of the bombings prior to 2003. Note that allegiance to resistance appeared to trump allegiance to religion. And most important, for bombers and for the publics that exalted them, the notion of self-sacrifice would not have existed except for the context: a perceived necessity for group defense.

Most Bombers Do Not Come from Extremist Institutions

2. Indoctrination: madrassas, mosques and terror cells manufacture suicide bombers. Indoctrination suggests brainwashing. In popular parlance it can happen emotionally, when intense bonds are forged in a cell-like setting, or ideologically, where students are exposed to one rigid view of the world. If such mechanisms have been at work in fomenting global terror, we should see it in the data. Bombers would: a) spend significant time "training" with terror organizations; b) exhibit organizational allegiance, and probably share political views with their mentoring institutions; and c) come disproportionately from extremist madrassas or mosques. Above all, we would expect to locate the genesis of the twenty-first century surge in martyrdom in such institutions. But this is not what we find.

Consider the lack of organizational attachments revealed in a 2003 study of 15 would-be Palestinian bombers in the second intifada. Sixty percent had no prior experience with terror organizations, much less a history of violence against Israel. Twenty percent started their mission within one week of accepting it, while 80 percent set out on their mission within a month. Indeed, half of them volunteered for missions, while those recruited were usually approached to take on the mission by family or friends. Organizational allegiance was slim: 20 percent originally attempted missions independently, turning to local groups to help them when matériel or logistics became difficult. Three switched organizations when it appeared another group had better capabilities. These num-

Suicide Terrorist Campaigns, 1980–2003

Date	Terrorists	Completed Campaigns Religion	Target Country	# Attacks
1. 1983	Hezbollah	Islam	United States, France	5
2. 1982–1985	Hezbollah	Islam	Israel	11
3. 1985–1986	Hezbollah	Islam	Israel	20
4. 1990–1994	LTTE	Hindu/secular	Sri Lanka	15
5. 1995–2000	LTTE	Hindu/secular	Sri Lanka	54
6. 1994	Hamas	Islam	Israel	2
7. 1994–1995	Hamas	Islam	Israel	9
8. 1995	BKI	Sikh	India	1
9. 1996	Hamas	Islam	Israel	4
10. 1997	Hamas	Islam	Israel	3
11. 1998	PKK	Islam/secular	Turkey	3
12. 1999	PKK	Islam/secular	Turkey	11
13. 2001	LTTE	Hindu/secular	Sri Lanka	6

continued

Suicide Terrorist Campaigns, 1980–2003 [CONTINUED]

Ongoing Campaigns, as of December 2003

Date	Terrorists	Religion	Target Country	# Attacks
14. 1996–	al-Qaeda	Islam	United States, Allies	21
15. 2000–	Chechens	Islam/secular	Russia	19
16. 2000–	Kashmirs	Islam	India	5
17. 2000–	Several	Islam/secular	Israel	92
18. 2003–	Iraqi rebels	Unknown	United States, Allies	20
		Attacks Not Part of Organized Campaigns		14
Total incidents				315

LTTE = Liberation Tigers of Tamil Eelam
BKI = Babbar Khalsa International
PKK = Kurdistan Workers' Party

TAKEN FROM: Robert Pape, *Dying to Win: The Strategic Logic of Suicide.* Random House, 2005, p. 13.

bers, which ran parallel to findings in a similar Israeli government study, suggest that bomber convictions in the second intifada existed with little or no organizational priming. Terror organizations served as facilitators, not indoctrinators. Most bombers came to them through friends, and many times, friends engaged in operations together.

Neither organizational recruitment nor madrassa training figured heavily in former intelligence officer Marc Sageman's 2004 study of 172 members of the global Salafi jihad. Sageman found that discipleship, a kind of mentor-student indoctrination, accounted for only 8 percent of the network. Although the study included networks from Europe, the Mideast, the Maghreb, and Asia, that entire 8 percent came from only two Islamic boarding schools in Indonesia and Malaysia.

The remaining network came to jihad informally through kinship and friendship bonds, 20 and 70 percent respectively. Like the Palestinian case, many joined in groups. Importantly, 78 percent of the network joined jihad in a country other than their homeland. Many of them met in mosques—the primary local community centers for Muslims. Alienated and alone, they bonded over a feeling of Muslim victimhood as observed on television and in pictures of wars involving Muslims. Religious devotion did increase for most individuals prior to their missions, but it is difficult to say what that means: growing devotion could be a cause or an effect of engaging the jihadi network.

How does this compare to what we see in Iraq? Little evidence is available, but according to Saudi and Israeli investigations of 154 foreign fighters in Iraq, "The largest group [of foreign fighters] is young kids who see the images [of war] on TV and are reading the stuff on the Internet. Or they see the name of a cousin on the list or a guy who belongs to their tribe, and they feel a responsibility to go." This suggests that foreign fighters come self-motivated, ready to sacrifice before funneling themselves into insurgent networks within the country.

What of hate-preaching madrassas throughout the Muslim world? Consider Pakistan, known as a "Jihad U" of sorts, with its ten thousand-plus madrassas, many of them sending students to Afghanistan for the war there. We would expect Pakistan to produce bombers in the early stages of global jihad, but there were only two. Rigid worldviews were not enough to push students to strap on bombs. They needed an emotional impetus. One had existed in Afghanistan; another was with the invasion of Iraq. Images of humiliation and needless death were ubiquitous on television, and in stories from friends and family. By the end of 2004, the number of Pakistani martyrs reached at least 10.

In sum, until 2004 and despite their hate-mongering, religious institutions did not contribute significantly to the rise in global terror. Instead, the empirical data parallel neuroscientific inquiries into how people acquire beliefs: First, emotion and social ties precede acquisition of ideology; second, joining the jihad does not appear to be an explicit decision, but a social and emotional process that happens over time.

Identifying the Target of Terrorism

3. *Terrorists justify their violence with the language of Islam.* What about Islamic texts and martyr statements? By designating the non-Muslim West as an infidel enemy, do they not endorse a "we hate you for who you are, not what you do" belief? A closer examination of three words—infidel, jihad, and martyr—calls this into question.

Abu Bakr Ba'asyir may be the most qualified "zealot" to teach about infidels. As the Emir of Jema'ah Islamiyya in Indonesia (an affiliate of al Qaeda), he is arguably responsible for at least 202 deaths, many from the Bali bombings in October 2002. But he says the logic of jihad is not against nonbelievers: "There are two types of infidels; the infidel who is against Islam and declares war on Islam is called *kafir harby* [enemy infidel]. The second type is *kafir dhimmi* [protected infidel]. These are people who don't fight against Islam, but don't embrace Islam or remain neutral. . . . As long as other communities don't fight against [us], we won't fight them." Ba'asyir says that the people in power today "do not tolerate [Islam], as in the case of America now which pushes its idea to change Islam with its weapons and dollars."

What does it mean to "fight" against Islam, and is the U.S. guilty? If "fighting" Islam means dictating what is preached in mosques, or disallowing headscarves in France, it was happening long before today. By itself, religious and cultural infringement on Islam was not enough to spur individuals to the risk and sacrifice of jihadi terror.

Rather, it seems that most Muslims, including terrorists, justify defensive jihad in response to violent social injustices. For instance, Osama bin Laden's statements are shrouded in religious references, but he cites the persecution of Islam in communal terms: "Its sons are being killed, its blood is being shed, its holy places are being attacked." Such are the images and arguments that accompany most bomber wills and videos. Such are the images invoked in polling questions that ask whether Islam is under "threat": Moderate Muslims who respond in the affirmative tend to support terror against the West.

Justifying Jihad and Martyrdom

The Islamic debate over jihad—greater and lesser, collective vs. individual, offensive vs. defensive, and ethical concerns—is too complex to capture here. But most of those joining jihad today have not captured it either. They are not religious scholars, and the jihad that originally appeals to them appeals on the emotional basis of defense. The jihadi narrative solves a pressing emotional problem: Why are my people dying, or oppressed? What can I do?

In Palestine, psychologist Brian Barber found that adolescent participation in the struggle against occupation is correlated with higher esteem and pro-social in-group behavior, despite its risks and sacrifices. In contrast, unorganized Bosnian Muslim youth studied during the Balkans conflict exhibited lower self-esteem, antisocial behavior, and general feelings of depression. Irrespective of the chances for success, in certain conditions it may be psychologically harder to not act.

We know that suicide bombing and jihad are statistically unlikely where there are civil liberties and constructive political channels for action. That said, even in democratic countries opportunity is a matter of perception. Thus wrote Mohammad Khan before he became the leader of the London bombers, "Our words have no impact upon you. Therefore I'm going to talk to you in language that you will understand. Our words are dead until we give them life with our blood." In short, emotions matter to the creation and embrace of radical beliefs, especially the beliefs worth dying for. "Emotions create new beliefs . . . [because they] entail an appraisal based on currently salient concerns."

In Arabic, the root for martyr has two meanings. Westerners know the term in its offensive sense: those who "sacrifice their lives"—often against us—in jihad (*istish'hadiyyin*). But the foundational meaning is "those who are killed by the enemy" (*shuhada*)—often noncombatants, i.e., civilian casualties. The distinction is important because most terrorists and their communities will tell you that in the locale, state or homeland they identify with, *shuhada* (innocent casualties) came before the *istish'hadiyyin* (bombers). Whether or not they agree with the tactic of terror, these populations understand the *istish'hadi* as giving his life for those who fell before, and to prevent those who would fall in the future.

Those who interview terrorists often hear about the role that media images have played in their conclusions that Muslims are threatened. A militant in Gaza once remarked to me about the power of television: "The difference between the first intifada and the second is television. Before, I knew when we were attacked here, or in a nearby camp, but the reality of the attacks everywhere else was not so clear. Now, I cannot get away from Israel—the TV brings them into my living room. . . . And you can't turn the TV off. How could you live with yourself? At the same time, you can't ignore the problem—what are you doing to protect your people? . . . We live with an internal struggle. Whether you choose to fight or not, every day is this internal struggle."

For all of us, images we view on television prompt two separate processes: affective reactions and cognitive appraisals. We feel the characters on-screen, but the feelings are turned off with an appraisal of reality. If the images were of your group under attack, however, it is highly plausible they would remain salient. We see this in the new terror. Global jihadis, like 78 percent of Sageman's network, often don't come from war zones. Like descriptions of Iraqi foreign fighters, they see images of injustice, have friends or family there, and feel obligated to help.

Social Motivations Are More Powerful than Religious Ones

Religious beliefs do not simply mold individuals. They exist as "sets of ideas that 'are there,' as if on the shelves of a supermarket waiting for someone to make them their own." Individuals pull them off the shelf when their old frames no longer make sense of the world around them.

If beliefs are not born of sacred texts alone, neither are behaviors like marytrdom. Rather, would-be bombers place jihadi values—fighting for life, dignity, equality—above all else.

It is not the commandment that is sacred, but the emotional reward it bestows.

We need to be asking new questions: For what are normal individuals able to kill? A plausible answer is: their community, under threat. When does a person make costly sacrifices to do so? Within a social structure—terror cell, a military unit, a family, or group of friends—that continually regenerates conviction to a cause, a feeling of obligation to do something about it, and a sense of shame at the idea of letting each other down. Whether one lands in a social group with jihadi tendencies may be random. But the prerequisite for this path is perceived injustice.

Periodical Bibliography

The following articles have been selected to supplement the diverse views presented in this chapter.

Shahid Afsar, Chris Samples, and Thomas Wood	"The Taliban: An Organizational Analysis," *Military Review*, May–June 2008.
Nadwa Arar	"Muslim Fundamentalism a Threat to the West?" *World & I*, November 1, 2008.
Scott Atran	"The Moral Logic and Growth of Suicide Terrorism," *Washington Quarterly*, Spring 2006.
Tony Blair	"A Battle for Global Values," *Foreign Affairs*, January–February 2007.
Philip Jenkins	"Clerical Terror," *New Republic*, December 24, 2008.
Alan B. Krueger and Jitka Maleckova	"Education, Poverty and Terrorism: Is There a Causal Connection?" *Journal of Economic Perspectives*, Fall 2003.
Ziauddin Sardar	"The Terror of Self-Satisfaction," *New Statesman*, April 23, 2007.
Lazar Stankov, Gerard Saucier, and Goran Knezevic	"Militant Extremist Mind-Set: Proviolence, Vile World, and Divine Power," *Psychological Assessment*, March 2010.
Sarah Stern	"The Wahhabi Jihad for Young American Minds," *inFocus Quarterly*, Winter 2008.
Omer Taspinar	"Fighting Radicalism, Not 'Terrorism': Root Causes of an International Actor Redefined," *SAIS Review*, Summer–Fall 2009.

OPPOSING
VIEWPOINTS®
SERIES

CHAPTER 3

How Can Extremism Be Countered?

Chapter Preface

A key question on the topic of extremism is whether it is possible for the attitudes and behaviors of extremists to change or whether the only way to counter extremism is by using force. A study called "Personal Transformations: Moving from Violence to Peace," prepared by psychologist Renee Garfinkel, was documented in a special report in April 2007 for the United States Institute of Peace. For this study, Garfinkel interviewed people in regions of conflict around the world who were once religious extremists and who are now working for peaceful change. Garfinkel reports the following:

> One of the key psychological characteristics of extremism is black-and-white thinking: ascribing goodness to one's own group and projecting evil onto the other. The culture of extremism contains language, stories, and reasoning that contribute to the demonization of the other. This "us and them" mentality has been documented in a great range of extremist cultures, including those that have led to genocide. . . .
>
> In religious extremism, the projection of evil onto the other is expressed in transcendent terms that imbue hate with cosmic significance. Images of God and the devil, for example, are handy and serviceable. This splitting of the world into good and evil is one of the most fundamental assumptions that our interviewees challenged in their journey to peacemaking. Recognizing the shared humanity of the enemy was a necessary, but often very difficult, step.

According to Garfinkel, it is at the individual level—when one person observes common characteristics of humanity in the face or life of his enemy—that change from extremism to pacifism takes place. Garfinkel compares the experience to a spiritual conversion.

Others believe that extremism needs to be curtailed by legislation. Russia passed a law in 2002 that counters extremist activities by forbidding organizations and individuals from committing a number of acts, including terrorist activities; inciting racial, ethnic or religious strife and social discord associated with violence or calls for violence; vandalism motivated by ideological, political, racial, national, or religious hatred; and spreading propaganda that claims exclusivity, superiority, or inferiority of citizens according to their attitude toward their religious, social, racial, ethnic, religious, or linguistic background. An organization found conducting such activities must cease these behaviors or the organization may be required to disband. This law is being used against various extremist factions including neo-Nazis, antigay groups, and Islamic terrorists.

The United States also uses legal means to combat extremism. Laws against extremist activities, often referred to as "hate crimes," increase the punishment a person receives if the crime committed is "motivated, in whole or in part, by the offender's bias against a race, religion, sexual orientation, ethnicity/ national origin, or disability and are committed against persons, property, or society." Unlike Russia, the United States punishes the individuals who commit these crimes rather than the organizations with which they are affiliated.

These are just a few of the many perspectives on how extremism can be countered. The viewpoints in this chapter consider whether it is possible for extremists to change and examine a number of ways in which extremism might be countered.

| "The most powerful weapon against Islamists and jihadists is to create public spaces in which former extremists can discuss why they entered Islamist networks and why they left."

Extremists Can Be Persuaded to Change

Ed Husain

Ed Husain spent five years as part of the Islamist organization Hizb ut-Tahrir. He wrote a book, The Islamist, *which explains why he left the organization, and he actively works to defeat Islamism, especially in his native Great Britain. In the following viewpoint, he explains why he believes that the best way to combat Islamism is for former Islamists to speak out.*

As you read, consider the following questions:

1. How does Husain explain the difference between Islam and Islamism?
2. What happened to former Islamist Hassan Butt? Why?
3. What does Husain say is accomplished when former Islamists speak out and are given public spaces in which to do so?

Ed Husain, "If Words Could Kill Me," *New Statesman*, June 18, 2007, p. 18. Copyright © 2007 New Statesman, Ltd. Reproduced by permission.

I thought Britain was a free and civilized country where I would no longer hear talk of public executions—I used to live in Saudi Arabia, where weekly, public beheadings are the norm. I was wrong. There is an unchallenged, unreported Islamist underworld in the UK [United Kingdom] in which talk of jihad, bombings, stabbings, killings and executions is usual. Rhetoric is an indication of a certain mind-set and, I believe, the prelude to terror.

In my book, *The Islamist*, I try to reclaim Islam from Islamism and separate the ancient spiritual path from a postcolonial political ideology. Condemnation of the book, mainly by Islamists, has not ceased for over a month.

In Manchester in April [2007], Hassan Butt, a one-time jihadist who is now opposed to extremism, was stabbed and beaten for speaking out against fanaticism. He now lives in hiding. Why was this not reported in the mainstream media?

Islamists Use Cyberspace to Promote Their Message

The Islamist underworld is assisted greatly by cyberspace—from Baghdad to Birmingham, Islamists and their jihadist twin brothers exchange information and coded messages on the Web. Before Hassan's stabbing, his interview with an American media outlet condemning terrorism had been circulated on the Web.

In Internet chat rooms and discussion threads the Islamists break news of beheadings in Iraq, the downing of US helicopters and discuss who is next on their agenda of killing and destruction. The mainstream media is bewilderingly unaware of this fast-moving, influential underworld.

But things took an uglier turn recently. Showkat Ali, a member of Hizb ut-Tahrir, who is training in Birmingham to become a schoolteacher, wrote a rap-like poem and posted it on several prominent Muslim Web sites. He wrote that his poem "was inspired by several Muslims who have betrayed Islam and the Ummah and are now openly working for the Crusader West in its losing battle against Political Islam". Purporting to speak my mind and likening me to Judas, he wrote:

No ifs no Butts [Hassan Butt]

Some people after me

To stab me in the heart

Like they did Hassan in Manchester

I dread the return of the Caliphate

Who will apply to extradite me

Put me on trial

And then execute me

As a traitor.

I believe the above lines are a coded call for my death, written in the first-person narrative to absolve Ali and his organisation from any responsibility.

I was once involved with Hizb ut-Tahrir and know from first hand the games it plays. The Hizb raise the political temperature, manipulate violent rhetoric and then create the climate for others to pull the trigger. I saw this happen on my college campus in Newham in 1995, when Ayotunde Obunabi was killed as a result of the supremacist, jihadist, racist milieu the Hizb fostered on campus. Soon, on a larger scale, the Hizb gave birth to al-Muhajiroun, whose members and associates bombed Tel Aviv in 2003, London in 2005 and plan other atrocities that the security services continue to monitor. How much longer will we tolerate the rhetoric of jihadism in our midst?

The Best Weapon Against Terrorism

In my experiences of living in Saudi Arabia in the aftermath of the 2004 and 2005 terrorist attacks in Riyadh and Jeddah, the most powerful weapon against Islamists and jihadists is to create public spaces in which former extremists can discuss

Extremists Must Be Persuaded by Values

This is ultimately a battle about modernity. Some of it can be conducted and won only within Islam itself. But let us remember that extremism is not the true voice of Islam. Millions of Muslims the world over want what all people want: to be free and for others to be free. They regard tolerance as a virtue and respect for the faith of others as a part of their own faith.

This is a battle of values and for progress, and therefore it is one that must be won. If we want to secure our way of life, there is no alternative but to fight for it. That means standing up for our values, not just in our own countries but the world over. We need to construct a global alliance for these global values and act through it. Inactivity is just as much a policy, with its own results. It is simply the wrong one.

Islamist extremism's whole strategy is based on a presumed sense of grievance that divides people against one another. Our answer has to be a set of values strong enough to unite people with one another. This is not just about security or military tactics. It is about hearts and minds, about inspiring people, persuading them, showing them what our values stand for at their best.

Tony Blair, "A Battle for Global Values,"
Foreign Affairs, *January–February 2007.*

why they entered Islamist networks and why they left. This removes the impenetrable mystique of these networks. It opens up their underworld. On Saudi television, former Islamists and jihadists recounted in detail why they abandoned the jihadist wing of Wahhabism, or al-Qaeda.

This scrutiny of extremism gives the public a better understanding of radicalisation, terror and its ideological underpinnings. More importantly, it gives people hope that we can together defeat this cancer in our midst. It also prevents a new generation of young Muslims from trying to walk the path that I traversed.

When courageous young men like Butt are stabbed and the media and authorities remain silent, it gives the wrong signal to those inside extremist organisations who are considering leaving. The rhetoric of "betrayal" also silences moderate Muslims who fear reprisals for speaking out, one reason that Muslim condemnation of extremism in Britain has been relatively low key. When coded death threats appear on popular Muslim Web sites, it prevents the emergence of a robust public space in which former Islamists can demolish the psychological confidence of extremists. To speak out against Islamism is not betrayal, it is fidelity to Islam and humanity. In the Quran, God refers to ennobling *bani adam*, or humanity. Ours is not a tribal religion. To condemn and dissociate from Islamism in all its forms is a religious duty, as illustrated by the words and actions of the majority of the world's Muslim scholars, from al-Azhar in Egypt to Deoband in India.

Islam Is Good for Britain—Islamists Are Not

In Britain, the differences between Islamism and Islam have been blurred to the extent that many Muslims fail to draw the distinction, as do large numbers of us on the left. Mistakenly, we sympathise with those who articulate anti-American, anti-war, pro-Palestinian grievances, without realising that Islamists of the entryist school are not allies of the left, but sworn enemies with a long history of terrorism against leftists in, among other countries, Algeria, Palestine and Bangladesh. We should know our Muslim from our Islamist. Just as we don't talk to the BNP [the right-wing British National Party] to understand white, working-class grievances, we need not engage with Islamists to comprehend Muslim suffering.

Islam, with its history of plurality and spirituality, has a natural home in Britain. Islamism, a political ideology set up to confront the West, does not. Today, it is talk of execution of moderate Muslims; unless we stem the rising tide of radical Islamist rhetoric in Britain, a prelude to jihadism, then the carnage of Baghdad may well erupt in Bradford and Birmingham.

> "If our time is to be limited, it would be nice to see less of it wasted on pleas for Muslim grown-ups—or anybody else—to get inside the heads of their militant mutineers with a view to gentle persuasion."

Extremists Cannot Be Persuaded to Change

Carol Sarler

Carol Sarler is a British journalist. In the following viewpoint, she considers the deep-rooted disagreements she observes between various denominations of Christian fundamentalists. Using the Christians as an example, she concludes that British "moderate" Muslims will not be able to persuade extremists to change their perspective because strong religious views cannot be changed by persuasion.

As you read, consider the following questions:

1. Why does Sarler believe her atheist family is able to communicate with the various Christian groups better than Christians communicate with each other?

2. Why does Sarler say that when it comes to matters of faith and belief division must happen?

3. Sarler talks about former jihadists who have become "moderate Muslims." What does she say about the way they became moderates and why they won't be able to influence other jihadists?

Funny the difference a few weeks can make. When I went away for an extended holiday, the subtle but unmistakable consensus on the threat to life and limb was more or less as it had been for some years: that jihadists [who champion holy war] are rotten fellows, but only small in number when compared with the 'vast majority' of 'moderate Muslims' who are, of course, not culpable. At all. Of anything. Ever.

When I came back, the consensus had shifted. Now, it appears, they might be a teeny bit worthy of blame after all—not for the violence itself, but for failing to keep their hotheads in line. Headlines are thundering: 'We need Muslims to do more', 'Muslims have to join this battle' and 'Muslims must raise their voices in anger'. It's been the battle cry of the summer [of 2007] so far—we demand that moderate Muslims persuade, cajole and convince their radicals, for all the world as if they can actually do as we ask.

The fact is, even if they would, there's not a virgin's chance in paradise that they could; you might as well have asked [Irish radio personality] Terry Wogan to rein in the IRA [Irish Republican Army]. And nothing illustrates the inherent difficulties better than, if you will indulge me, reflections on my recent sojourn.

Christian Fundamentalists Disagree on Everything

To wile away time in the American Bible Belt, as I do for many months of each year, is to witness Christian fundamentalism at its fruitiest, nuttiest, rancorous best. On our little coastal Georgia island it is a proud boast that there are more churches than bars, while clever sleight of county planning ensures it will stay that way; no hard liquor licence may be given to premises within 500 yards of a house of the Gud Lawd and upon that all are agreed. They don't, however, agree on anything else.

Episcopalians fight with Lutherans who tussle with Presbyterians who despair of Methodists; the First Baptists do not speak to the Second Baptists and neither is on terms with the First Free Will Baptists (jokes about the oxymoronic nature of which do not play well; you may trust me on that). At your peril shall you confuse the Church of God with the Church of the Son of God and we should be grateful for St Williams, up on Frederica Road, because at least the others can unite in their hatred of its Roman Catholic congregation.

Notably, however, nobody appears to have a problem with us. The unfamiliarity of our atheism stirs occasional curiosity, but beyond that there is nothing they can do with it; it cannot serve as a source of dialogue, for what would we discuss? Does God exist? No. Life—at least for those of us unburdened by rumours of an eternity—is just too short.

Christian Fundamentalists Can Get Along with Atheists

The Sarlers' interaction with the local people, therefore, is often a good deal more straightforward than they manage with each other. Without the possibility of a wrangle over the commandments of a deity, we seek common ground in a shared understanding of the more prosaic laws of Man; you do not, for instance, need to debate the evangelism of the snake handler to tell him that if that poor serpent is so much as a squished mouse short of a decent supper, you'll call on animal welfare.

It's not so much fun, of course, without the spice of scoring points—though to be fair, while it is easy to take the mick

Moral Outrage Motivates Religious Extremists

As an observation from interviewing terrorists and those who inspire and care for them, individuals who opt for suicide attacks often seem motivated by values and small-group dynamics that trump rational self-interest. Violation of such values leads to moral outrage and seemingly irrational vengeance ("get the offender, even if it kills us"). Adherence to sacred values, which provides the moral foundations and faith of every society or sect that has endured for generations, ultimately leads to perceived moral obligations that appear to be irrational, such as martyrdom. One is obliged to act "independently of the likelihood of success," as in acts of heroism or terrorism, because believers could not live with themselves if they did not.

When our research team interviews would-be suicide bombers and their sponsors and when we survey their supporters, for example, Hamas students or students in Indonesian madrassas that have produced suicide bombers, we pose questions such as, "What if your family were to be killed in retaliation for your action?" or "What if your father were dying and your mother discovered your plans and asked you to delay until the family could recover?" Almost all answer along the lines that, although duty to family exists, duty to God cannot be postponed. The typical response to the question "What if your action resulted in no one's death but your own?" is, "God will love you just the same."

Scott Atran, *"The Normal Logic and Growth of Suicide Terrorism,"* Washington Quarterly, *Spring 2006.*

out of the fissures of faith in the Deep South, they are not unique. A few weeks ago news reached us even there of some tussle between British bishops wherein, and I hope I have this right, one pointed to the horrors of climate change while another claimed it was raining because God was cross; meanwhile, the pope was making mischief with his declaration that Protestants aren't 'proper' Christians.

All ideology is prone to such division. I once had friends in the Communist Party of Britain (Marxist-Leninist), membership of which never swelled much beyond seven—but all seven were in fervent accord that while we in the wider world deserved their disdain, their most visceral contempt should be kept for all members of any Communist Party that did not append the crucial, bracketed (M-L). In other words, it should be kept not for those who completely refused to share their doctrine, but for those who very nearly did.

When it comes to matters of faith and belief, it is not simply that the division tends to happen; it is that, surely, it must happen. As already declared, I come at this from the outside so, please, be gentle; still, it seems to me axiomatic that if you believe there is one god, and that this god has made available to you one scripture, then all beyond that—language being the inexact medium that it is—is interpretation. The inevitable problem, therefore, is that a thousand interpretations of one god's one word mean 999 misinterpretations by people who read it and got it wrong; apostates could scarcely be worse! No wonder our First Baptists dine more easily with us than with their Seconds; he who has not read, let alone studied, the Holy Book cannot commit the offence (in every sense of the word) of traducing it.

Muslim Fundamentalists Can't Be Persuaded by Talk

But if this is clear instance of something that is observable worldwide—why should it not apply to British Muslims? If one man's reading of the Koran instructs military jihad [holy war], it is absurdly presumptuous to expect that instruction to be overturned by those who read the same text but 'failed' to understand its message; few of us, after all, are inclined to be swayed by those to whom we feel superior.

There is a slew of young men currently writing in newspapers about how they used to be jihadists but have now seen the error of their ways and become 'moderate Muslims'; each charts slow self-realisation of their own idiocy, rather than a peaceable conversion wrought by a sensible chat over a cuppa with an elder from a warmer, fuzzier mosque than their usual blast-happy haunt.

Whether the folly or the world will end first is not, at the moment, a happy bet. But if our time is to be limited, it would be nice to see less of it wasted on pleas for Muslim grown-ups—or anybody else—to get inside the heads of their militant mutineers with a view to gentle persuasion. The only understanding likely to be productive is of the kind needed for sufficient intelligence to catch them and thwack them; in short, as with the decision not to engage with the snake handlers, less of the word of God, with which one may disagree, and more of the laws of Man, with which one may not. At least we all know what they are and even (especially?) within the tension of terrorist threat, they are open to absolutely no interpretation at all.

> *"In the face of sociological, cultural, psychological problems, the Islamic world has no other answer but the religious answer."*

Fundamentalist Islamic Schools Teach Extremism

Samir Khalil Samir

Samir Khalil Samir is an Egyptian Catholic priest who teaches Arab and Islamic studies at Saint Joseph University in Beirut. In the following viewpoint, Samir contends that traditional Islamic schools, called madrassas, teach fundamentalism that leads to terrorism. He believes that the way Islam and the Koran are taught in these schools does not provide a way for Muslims to relate to the non-Muslim world other than to fight against it.

As you read, consider the following questions:

1. What does Samir say are the two problems in Islamic teaching?
2. Why does Samir say Muslims need an Enlightenment?
3. What distinction does Samir say Muslims do not accept, and what does he say would happen if they discovered this distinction?

Samir Khalil Samir, "Islamic Terrorism: A Result of What Is Being Taught at Madrassas," *AsiaNews*, September 8, 2005. Reproduced by permission. www.asianews.it and desk@asianews.it.

Terrorism is not the unexpected result of Islam, but the direct result of what is being taught at madrassas, traditional schools. And not only because many schools give training in terrorism and guerrilla warfare, but mainly because they educate in fundamentalism. They depict religion as the solution to any problem and look at the world and the West in an intransigent and radical way, through which the only solution is jihad [holy war], the destruction of the West and all that seems to conspire against religion.

Any fight against terrorism must take steps to change the traditionalist educational process which is in the hands of imams [religious leaders] and which they are spreading throughout the world. I had the chance to meet the famous imam of Qatar, Yusuf [al-]Qaradawi: He is an intelligent and good man, open to dialogue with Christians. There is a lot, however, about him that is fundamentalistic. To give just one example, he justifies, without the least bit of concern, terrorist attacks against the people of Israel. [Al-]Qaradawi speaks every day on Qatari television, for over an hour, broadcasting his mentality. Like him, thousands of imams are teaching without much training and without having assimilated human sciences.

Islamic Teaching Presents Problems

There are two problems in Islamic teaching: In the first place, there is no recognized central authority. Not even Al-Azhar, Cairo's illustrious university, is recognized by everyone. Thus imams and muftis (those who declare fatwas, juridical rulings) exist by the thousands. One has but to study a bit of Koran to claim status as a mufti. At one time, 30 years ago, this was not the case: Each country had at most one mufti recognized by the entire nation. Instead, today, all imams claim to be muftis and each have their own followers.

The other problem is the teaching done by the ulemas (scholars, men of learning). In actual fact, these ulemas are "men of learning" only in one limited field: They have learned the Koran by heart, they have learned the thousands of sayings attributed to Mohammad; they have memorized thousands of the juridical rulings of a large number of imams. But they have never studied math, sociology, psychology, foreign literature, they are not able to read a book in a Western language. History is limited to the Islamic world; religions are studied only as a function of how to respond if Islam is criticized. It is a kind of study which is very restricted and closed in on itself. Al-Azhar University itself and all others in the world are characterized by this closed quality. They are therefore unable to analyze Western cultures, unable to understand situations that are different from those where Islam makes up the majority. And, in the end, they are unable to understand the world of Muslim Europe: Their criteria are valid only for an Islamic world where everyone is Muslim. They are able to understand only this type of medieval situation. They cannot understand a secular society like Turkey. They wish therefore to label everything as Islamic: banks, politics, science, medicine, etc.

When these imams arrive in the West, more than 90% of them at work in Western Europe do not speak the local language: They speak only Arabic, or Turkish, etc. They are detached from the culture of the country in which they actually live. So what can they possibly say to the young Muslims born in England, France, Germany? They can only repropose a medieval system, perhaps even updated, but they cannot work toward modernizing Islam, reproposing the split between religion and modern society.

There is no link between the normal studies done by a young Westerner and the studies done by their imams. It would be as if Catholic priests wished to evangelize the world studying just the Bible from the perspective of ancient considerations.

Islamic Fundamentalism Attracts Troubled Youth

This explains why young people, educated within modernity, carried out terrorist acts in London. Most of them were and are normal youths, born in Great Britain. Then, inner troubles took them within range of those who preach fundamentalism. From Great Britain, they went to Pakistan to be educated in a madrassa (school). Essentially, they were trained in fundamentalism. Everyone says: It's their right. But by analyzing this classical Muslim teaching, one can see that terrorism stems right from the type of education offered by these madrassas.

I repeat: Terrorism stems from the type of education that they give—traditional Muslim religious teaching, which is the most widespread. In the madrassas, in Islamic teaching, the typical dissatisfaction of every young person finds an immediate and easy answer in religion. In the face of sociological, cultural, psychological problems, the Islamic world has no other answer but the religious answer. For example, instead of analyzing a problem from the political point of view, instead of fighting, perhaps even together with Christians and atheists, to bring about justice, they might say: We are fighting in the name of Islam.

Under such influence, young people, initially accustomed to wearing Western clothes, change their attire and take to wearing a white robe and head covering, and they let their beard grow. These correspond to just as many symbols of a changed mentality, of a rejection of the West, a crisis of identity and spiritual distress. Until 30 years ago, this did not happen—today it does. And having taken on these symbols means having entered into a fundamentalist, literalist way of thinking, and being prone to manipulation.

Pilgrimages to the Mecca are also an occasion for indoctrination in fundamentalism.

I know several Muslim ladies who were integrated very well into European society: They dressed in a Western manner, wore makeup, went out with their head uncovered. After a pilgrimage to the Mecca, they returned and took to putting on a veil, wearing a chador, asking for halal meat. . . .

It is difficult in the Islamic world to get out of the expected bounds of religion, but it's a necessary step.

Islam Needs to Recognize Secularity

An effort is needed so that secularity becomes part of the Islamic world. This concept is known by, at the most, a few Muslims educated in Western culture. In general, in the Islamic world, secularity does not exist. In Arabic, we have the word "secularity," 'almâniyya, a new term coined by Arab Christian, but very often it is confused with "atheism." Secularity must be, above all, affirmed in the interpretation of the Koran.

In my teaching at Saint Joseph University in Beirut, I taught various times a course on the Bible and the Koran. I told my students: Let's study these books as historical documents, from the point of view of history, philology, etc. With Christians, this can be done; but with Muslims, it is almost impossible. All this makes it difficult to understand historically the Koran and to grasp the original meaning . . . of the words. A few examples follow. We all know that the word "paradise" is of Persian origin, but for Islamic students and imams, this conclusion is unacceptable. The word "Evangelos (Good News)" derives from Greek, but for Muslim students and their imams, this is unacceptable: For them, the Koran descended directly from God and cannot have human or historical "encrustations." Therefore, if in the Koran one finds record of the annunciation to Mary, for Muslims it is impossible to deduce some kind of influence of the Christian world on the Koran. And if the two records contradict each other at

Madrasahs Lead Impressionable Youth to Terrorism

Currently, there are estimated to be several hundred thousand madrasahs [traditional Islamic schools] in operation. Young imams frequently found and administer madrasahs of their own in their hometowns and villages. Because the imam is often the only person in town who is literate and qualified to preside over daily prayers, weddings, funerals, festivals, and other rituals, he and his madrasah are accorded great respect, and they wield great influence.

Impressionable youth growing up in madrasahs whose imams espouse intolerant, violent teachings are prime recruits for extremist causes. Widespread reporting on such madrasahs and their teachers has led many in the West to see the schools as symbols of extreme Islam. Western descriptions typically reflect this. The *New York Times Magazine* has described the madrasah system as "education of the holy warrior." Writing in *Policy Analysis*, Andrew Coulson cleverly dubbed madrasahs "weapons of mass instruction." The 9/11 Commission Report referred to the schools as "incubators of violent extremism."

Todd Schmidt, *"Reforming the Madrasah,"*
Military Review, *May–June 2008.*

some point, the Koran's is without doubt more correct since "it was revealed by God in a complete way."

The only way out is to affirm that the Koran is a historical document, written by a human being, perhaps even religiously inspired.

This is why I always say that Muslims need an Enlightenment, in other words a revolution in thought that affirms the value of worldly reality in and of itself, detached from religion, though not in opposition to it. Scholars in Egypt have been publishing a series of books for some 30 years called al-Tanwîr, enlightenment, but the influence of Al-Azhar and the mullahs [Islamic clerics] is still too strong.

In speaking of Enlightenment, it is clear that we are speaking of an Enlightenment that does not renounce the religious element. On the other hand, perhaps the West needed to go through secularism in order to gain a new balance. By now, the Church in the West is not seen as an enemy, but as an element that contributes to civilization. And while there is a Christian humanism, recognized even by atheists, Islamic humanism does not exist. If an Islamic humanism is not developed, the distance between the modern world and the Muslim world will become abysmal.

There is technological and scientific modernization in the Islamic world, but this does not lead to a modern humanism. Many terrorists are people of a considerable cultural level; there are doctors, engineers, etc., among them. They have great scientific and technological culture, but they have not built a link between their science and religion. They take from the West the fruit, the technology, but they do not measure themselves up to the process that generated that fruit. The Western fruit of technology comes from a secularizing passage, first through Christianity, then by way of rationalism and Enlightenment. Muslims accept technology, but they do not accept the distinction between secular and religious. And this is wrong, as it does not generate a movement toward self-criticism and liberation.

If Muslims discovered this distinction, then they could dialogue with the West, criticize it, discern what is good in it and what is to be rejected. Instead, the lack of this distinction results in the total rejection of the West and in the plan for its destruction. Without recuperating secularity and the distinction between secular and religious, Islam is condemned to obscurantism.

"*Schools . . . can play a vital role in hammering out a new Muslim identity, one that combines being a good Muslim with being a good citizen in a pluralist society.*"

Islamic Schools Can Counter Extremism

Jay Tolson

In the following viewpoint Jay Tolson, a senior writer for U.S. News & World Report, considers how Islamic schools in Europe can help combat extremism and terrorism by teaching students to live in a multicultural society. He discusses one school in particular, Islamia Primary School in London, which makes an effort to teach students to be good British citizens as well as good Muslims.

As you read, consider the following questions:

1. How does Islamia's head teacher, Abdullah Trevathan, say that Muslim schools provide an antidote to Muslim extremism?

2. What does the author say may cause uneasiness about Muslim schools for many Britons?

Jay Tolson, "An Education in Muslim Integration," *U.S. News & World Report*, vol. 139, November 21, 2005, pp. 37, 38, 40. Copyright © 2005 U.S. News & World Report, L.P. Reproduced by permission.

3. According to Mohammed Mamdani, what does the Al-Sadiq school in London teach?

The riots that spread beyond the densely Muslim suburbs of Paris into other French cities and even into neighboring countries have confirmed many people's worst fears about growing alienation and extremism among the rising generation of Europe's roughly 14 million-member minority. To date [November 2005], at least, those riots say far more about the difficulties France and other European nations have had in integrating a largely Muslim underclass than they do about the rise of militant Islam in the West.

But beyond their obvious connection with race and social justice, the violent outbursts give pause to those who share French political scientist Gilles Kepel's view that the crucial struggle for Muslim minds is taking place not in the Arab world but in Europe. At the very least, the riots raise questions about the compatibility of liberal societies and Islam, challenging both the rigid secularism of many European liberals and the dogmatism of many European Muslims. And a number of those questions are being brought to a head in the arena of education, with debates raging about whether Islamic education is part of the problem of Muslim integration into European nations—or whether it might become part of the solution.

British Islamic School Teaches Pluralism

To Abdullah Trevathan, head teacher of north London's Islamia Primary School, a state-funded school that offers religious instruction and the study of Arabic along with the standard national curriculum, the answer is clear. Trevathan believes that schools such as Islamia—one of the first five Muslim faith schools to receive state funding in Britain—can play a vital role in hammering out a new Muslim identity, one that combines being a good Muslim with being a good citizen in a pluralist society.

That identity is clearly at odds with the one being pushed by Islamic extremists throughout Europe, often in innocent-seeming sports clubs or after-school Koran classes taught by Saudi-trained imams [religious leaders]. Their vision of Islam appeals to many of the second- or third-generation children of Pakistani, Turkish, or North African immigrants who crowd the ghetto-like neighborhoods of Europe's industrial cities and suburbs. Often raised in households where religion is a loose cultural matter, they are easily seduced by the austere Wahhabi-Salafist vision of a global community of the faithful living under strict Islamic law. Attracted by the moral absolutism, some are even drawn to the violent ways of the jihadists [those who wage holy war].

But how do Muslim schools provide an antidote to all of this? They do so, Trevathan and others argue, by exposing students to the classical Islamic traditions, whose richness was derived partly from their openness to changing cultural conditions. In addition, argues Asmat Ali, head of the girls' upper-school division of Islamia, Muslim schools give students confidence in their own Muslim identity, a confidence that makes them more at ease with their Britishness. And having a strong ethical and spiritual core arguably contributes to the academic success that Islamia and other faith schools enjoy. With over 97 percent of its upper-school graduates going on to enroll in a university, Islamia itself is, Trevathan says, "the most over-subscribed school in the UK [United Kingdom]."

Some Officials Criticize Islamic Schools

Despite the performance and promise of Muslim schools like Islamia, they are still the object of loud controversy in Britain. Possessing an established church, Britain has long provided government support for religious schools, and not just for Anglican ones. Today, out of a total of 22,000 state schools, some 7,000 are religious, all but 45 of which are associated with major Christian denominations. Yet the existence of five state-funded Muslim schools—with four more approved for support—has generated a seemingly disproportionate critical reaction. Several months before the July 7 [2005] subway bombing in London, England's chief school inspector criticized the curricula of Muslim schools and voiced concerns about their effect on national cohesion. Jonathan Romain, rabbi of a Reform synagogue in Maidenhead, England, and an outspoken critic of the entire principle of faith schools, echoes those concerns. "Whereas most clergy see faith schools as reinforcing values," he says, "I see them as dividing different communities." Romain is quick to add that he is not opposed to teaching about different faith traditions in religious education classes in normal state schools. But to create more faith schools is, he argues, "surely to see a problem arise in 30 years' time."

The uneasiness that many Britons feel about Muslim schools may stem from confusion about what these schools actually are. According to the Association of Muslim Schools in UK and Eire [Ireland], there are about 120 Islamic schools throughout Britain. But that figure includes everything from small Koranic academies to schools offering a full state curriculum and Islamic subjects. Fauzia Ahmad, a professor of sociology at the University of Bristol, says that this lack of differentiation "gives the impression that there are thousands of schools out there creating radicals."

While British citizenship is heavily emphasized at schools like Islamia, there is legitimate concern about what goes on in some of the others. Tariq Ramadan, a Swiss-born Muslim scholar who serves on a British task force on religious extremism, says that he approves faith schools "in principle" but is disturbed by schools—mainly those created explicitly for Muslim girls—whose real intention is to isolate the students from the rest of society. "I think we still have to assess every single school on what its project is."

Which, of course, is one good argument for bringing even more Muslim schools into the state-supported arrangement.

Not only does that guarantee that the school will offer a state-approved curriculum, but it also ensures some government oversight of the content of the religion classes. Yet some see such oversight as a potential problem. "There is a perception of Britain trying to shape a 'British Muslim,' which suggests a control aspect," says Ahmad, "and Muslims would not take kindly to that."

Many European Countries Face Similar Issues

Ultimately, though, the dilemma facing not just Britain but also Germany, the Netherlands, Spain, France, and Italy is broadly similar: If the European educational system does not play a constructive role in the religious education of devout European Muslims, then where will that education come from, and how will it be shaped? Part of Europe's difficulties today stems from the fact that most European imams and many of the Muslim leaders in prominent national organizations tend to be either religious conservatives or reactionaries—or simply out of touch with the rising generation of European Muslims. How can a new and visionary cadre of European Muslim leaders be created unless instruction in responsible and broad-minded Islam receives government support or at least government encouragement?

"What we have is a lack of leadership," says Mohammed Mamdani, a 22-year-old Sheffield-born Briton who founded the Muslim Youth Helpline to assist Muslim youths with personal and social problems. The members of the Muslim Council of Britain are, in his view, a typical graybeard lot, isolated from the larger British society and clueless about how Islam can play a positive role in helping young people to live in liberal, pluralistic societies. For his own relatively smooth adjustment to life as a young British Muslim, Mamdani gives considerable credit to the few years he spent in another north London Muslim school, Al-Sadiq. The school's approach to reconciling a strong Muslim ethos with the realities of living in a modern, liberal society is a model that he believes the British government should actively promote in other Muslim schools.

If Britain is moving at least quietly in that direction, so too are countries like the Netherlands, which has about 40 Muslim schools catering to about 3 percent of the nation's some 30,000 school-age Muslims. Those schools came under fierce criticism after a Muslim militant killed the controversial filmmaker Theo van Gogh. The Dutch government continues to support them, but, says Martine Soethout, member of a Ministry of Education task force on social cohesion: "Citizenship has been bolstered in all of them."

In Germany, home to some 3.5 million Muslims, many of the federal states have long left Islamic education in the hands of Turkish teachers, who instruct in Turkish and often follow curricula designed by Turkish diplomatic missions. But in recent years, one state has made Islamic studies a public school subject available to Muslim students, a development that led the University of Münster to adopt the subject as one of its teacher-training courses. Even in France, the citadel of strict church-state separation, the government provides money under a contractual arrangement for about 10 Muslim schools. And before the riots, the now much vilified French interior minister, Nicolas Sarkozy, was himself questioning his nation's rigid secularism as an obstacle to the ideal of an "Islam from France," not just an "Islam in France"—an ideal that includes a government-supported school for the training of imams.

The riots might even have given a boost to that kind of thinking, says Brandeis University scholar Jytte Klausen, author of a new book, *The Challenge of Islam*. About recent conversations with several European officials, she says, "Strangely, the riots are having the effect of convincing them that all the burden for integrating shouldn't rest on the shoulders of the

Muslim immigrants." Maybe there is reason to think that a long overdue Islamic reformation can still take off in Europe.

Periodical Bibliography

The following articles have been selected to supplement the diverse views presented in this chapter.

Nafeez Mosaddeq Ahmed — "Our Terrorists," *New Internationalist*, October 2009.

Christopher Boucek — "Saudi Arabia's 'Soft' Counterterrorism Strategy: Prevention, Rehabilitation, and Aftercare," Carnegie Endowment for International Peace, September 2008. www.carnegieendowment.org.

Michael Burleigh — "It's Time to Tackle Student Islamists," *Spectator*, January 27, 2010.

Babak Dehghanpisheh — "Retraining Terrorists: A Bold New Program in Iraq Uses Islam to Teach Insurgents the Error of Their Murderous Ways," *Newsweek International*, August 20, 2007.

Carol Dyer et al. — "Countering Violent Islamic Extremism: A Community Responsibility," *FBI Law Enforcement Bulletin*, December 2007.

Leslie H. Gelb — "Only Muslims Can Stop Muslim Terror," *Daily Beast*, January 7, 2010. www.thedailybeast.com.

Azeem Ibrahim — "Reducing Terrorism over the Long Term," Belfer Center for Science and International Affairs, October 27, 2008. http://belfercenter.ksg.harvard.edu.

Deepak Malhotra — "Without Conditions," *Foreign Affairs*, September–October 2009.

Susan Mohammed — "To Deprogram a Jihadist," *Maclean's*, February 2, 2009.

Umm Mustafa — "Why I Left Hizb ut-Tahrir," *New Statesman*, February 28, 2008.

OPPOSING
VIEWPOINTS®
SERIES

CHAPTER 4

How Is Extremism Apparent in the United States?

Chapter Preface

Extreme beliefs and behaviors are not confined to distant parts of the world. According to *Extremism in America*, an online document produced by the Anti-Defamation League,

> America unfortunately has no shortage of extremists. Some come from the Far Right, primarily in the form of racist and anti-Semitic hate groups or anti-government extremists. Others come from the Far Left, including environmental and animal rights extremists. Some extreme movements may focus around a single, narrow issue, such as abortion, and involve anti-abortion extremists who bomb health clinics. Other movements may stem from ideologies that stress racial superiority, fanatic religious beliefs, or radical political views. Whatever their origin or nature, many extremist movements have adherents who are so committed to their vision that they are willing to break the law and to use violence to achieve their goals.

As this document indicates, a number of movements in the United States can be characterized by their extreme actions. One example of a movement often described as *extremist* is the white supremacist movement. According to *West's Encyclopedia of American Law*, white supremacy groups are "organizations that believe the Caucasian race is superior to all other races and therefore seek either to separate the races in the United States or to remove all non-Caucasians from the nation." Probably the most well-known of these groups is the Ku Klux Klan. Others include the Aryan Nations, which has several sub-groups; the White Patriot Party; and the neo-Nazis.

Some members of these groups prefer to be called *White Separatists*, declaring that they are not interested in violence against other races, but only want to live separately from them. According to www.whiteseparatist.com, "White Separatists do not want to rule over, or oppress other races. White

Separatists prefer to live in white communities and want all races to be separate. White Separatists want to limit the influences of the other cultures on our own and are happy to let the other races decide how they will govern their own communities." Others take a more active, and often violent, role in promoting their beliefs by destroying people who are not members of the white race. A number of violent crimes have been attributed to the white supremacist movement, including a January 2009 murder of two people in Brockton, Massachusetts, and the June 2009 shooting of an African American guard at the Holocaust Museum in Washington, D.C.

There are a number of other movements in the United States whose members, like the white supremacists, have beliefs that could be considered extreme. The viewpoints in this chapter consider several of these movements and whether they deserve to be labeled as *extremist*.

| "The agenda of extreme animal rightists is crystal clear: end the use of all animals as food, clothing, pets, and subjects of medical research."

Extremist Animal Rights Activists Are Terrorists

P. Michael Conn and James V. Parker

Both P. Michael Conn and James V. Parker have worked at the Oregon National Primate Research Center, an animal-testing facility that attempts to use animals humanely in biomedical research. In the following viewpoint, Conn and Parker discuss the actions of extreme animal rights activists, some of whom they believe do fall into the category of terrorists because of the violent threats and attacks against biomedical researchers they facilitate.

As you read, consider the following questions:

1. What do the authors say animal rights extremists claim about using animal research for drug development? What do the authors themselves believe about this question?

2. What did members of the Animal Liberation Front intend to do to Dr. Lynn Fairbanks of UCLA?

3. According to a quote from Senator Orrin Hatch, what happens when research laboratories and universities are targeted?

For years we have laughed at the antics of people in some of the more extreme segments of the animal rights movement—groups like People for the Ethical Treatment of Animals (PETA). They put up billboards encouraging children to drink beer instead of milk and vilify fast-food chains for cooking veggie burgers on the same grill as meat. They even wrote to Oklahoma City bomber Timothy McVeigh urging him to stop the killing at his dinner plate and to request a vegetarian dinner for his last meal. All this sure gets the media's attention and sometimes even a chuckle from the public. Well, maybe it's time to stop laughing.

We may choose to ignore the poor taste of the animal rights movement in equating the Holocaust of World War II with the raising of broiler chickens or the "enslavement" of circus animals with the slavery of African Americans in the United States. But consider this curious candor from one animal rights leader, "The life of an ant and that of my child should be granted equal consideration." What does *that* mean?

Can we ignore this statement from PETA cofounder Alex Pacheco: "Arson, property destruction, burglary, and threat are 'acceptable crimes' when used for the animal cause"?

FBI [Federal Bureau of Investigation] special agent David Szady, referring to Earth Liberation Front [ELF], one extremist group of the animal rights movement, said, "Make no mistake about it, by any sense or definition [this] is a domestic terrorism group." Animal rightists are domestic terrorists?

In the short term and for most of us, there is no reason for the jitters. We are not the scientists who use animal models to unlock secrets of physiology that may improve our health. So far, they have been the primary targets of animal extremists' wrath—people like the two Oregon researchers whose homes and cars were vandalized last December [2007]. There is no indication that the extremists will, any time soon, go after you and me for eating a hamburger, keeping a pet, taking meds, or using a pacemaker.

What Is at Stake?

The inconvenient truth is that in the long term, and for all of us, there is cause for concern. The agenda of extreme animal rightists is crystal clear: end the use of all animals as food, clothing, pets, and subjects of medical research. Yet we live longer and healthier lives due to vaccinations, better drugs, and improved information about nutrition and disease prevention—longer lives are the result of animal research.

Noting the impact of these extremists on the nation's health agenda, famed heart surgeon and 2007 Congressional Gold Medal winner Michael DeBakey said, "It is the American public who will decide whether we must tell hundreds of thousands of victims of heart attacks, cancer, AIDS, and other dread diseases that the rights of animals supersede a patient's right to relief from suffering and premature death."

Clarifying definitions will provide a good basis for discussion.

The term *animal welfare* refers to the idea that humans have a responsibility to care for animals and look out for their well-being. Because seeking animal welfare is in line with what is noblest in human nature, it is sometimes called "acting humanely." Most reasonable people agree with this. Researchers reflect these values in subscribing to high-quality care for animals, something codified into law as the Animal Welfare Act. Federal regulations are in place to minimize pain and suffering in research. At the authors' place of employment, the Oregon National Primate Research Center, animals live longer lives than their counterparts in the wild, owing to high-quality food and excellent veterinary care. One sad truth is that our animals get better medical care and nutrition than do many children in the U.S.

Animal rights, sometimes used as shorthand for any concern for animals, really means the belief that animals, like humans, possess some inalienable rights. It is our view that while animals do not have such rights—rights and responsibilities are correlative, and animals are unable to take responsibility for their actions—it is our duty as humans and ethical researchers to care for them humanely, just as we care for our pets.

Animal extremists portray themselves as engaged in a "David against Goliath" struggle on behalf of animals, but are they the true animal welfarists? Hardly! In 2006 alone, PETA killed 2,981 dogs, cats, puppies, kittens, and other animals—an astonishing 97 percent of the animals left in their care, according to the group's own records supplied to the Virginia Department of Agriculture and Consumer Services (2006). For comparison, the Virginia Society for the Protection of Animals (which operates in Norfolk, Virginia, as does PETA) euthanized less than 2.5 percent of the 1,404 animals placed with them in 2006. While PETA collects tens of millions in donations by claiming to advocate for the welfare of animals, the group has actually killed 17,400 pets since 1998.

PETA's most recently available tax filing (according to Guidestar.org) lists nearly $30 million in income from contributions, gifts, and grants offered by individuals who may believe that it is actually an animal welfare organization that helps strays.

Support for Terrorism

Many of its donors are also unaware that PETA has provided cash to individuals who publicly engaged in a terrorist agenda. A few examples were provided by *Lewiston Morning Tribune* (Idaho) writer Michael Costello. "PETA donated $45,200 to

... ALF [Animal Liberation Front] terrorist Rodney Coronado's legal defense. (Coronado was convicted in connection with an arson attack at Michigan State University that caused $125,000 worth of damage and destroyed thirty-two years of research data. On December 14, 2007, in a federal court in San Diego, he entered a guilty plea to one count of distribution of information related to the assembly of explosives and other charges.) They also ... 'loaned' Coronado's father $25,000 dollars [*sic*], which to our knowledge, has not been repaid. In 1999, PETA gave $2,000 to David Wilson, a national 'ALF spokesperson.' ... And sure enough, PETA has contributed to the ALF's sister organization; according to its own IRS [Internal Revenue Service] filing, in 2000 PETA openly donated $1,500 to the Earth Liberation Front. The Federal Bureau of Investigation (FBI) calls ELF 'the largest and most active U.S.-based terrorist group.'"

PETA probably doesn't want its donors to know that. Instead, it directs outrage toward "vivisectors" falsely accused of cruelty to animals to incense donors into reaching more deeply into their pockets.

"We are complete press sluts," the PETA leadership has claimed. On that single issue, we agree with PETA.

Although PETA is careful not to openly embrace the assaults, vandalism, and threats perpetrated by some groups, it does not oppose such violence either. Speaking of one animal extremist group whose leaders have been convicted of animal terrorism, PETA president Ingrid Newkirk said, "More power to SHAC [Stop Huntingdon Animal Cruelty] if they can get someone's attention."

The Animal Liberation Front can speak for itself, however. Says one of its leaders, Tim Daley, "In a war you have to take up arms and people will get killed, and I can support that kind of action by gasoline bombing and bombs under cars, and probably at a later stage, the shooting of vivisectors on their doorsteps. It's a war, and there's no other way you can stop vivisectors." Jerry Vlasak, head of the ALF press office, is equally candid, "I don't think you'd have to kill—assassinate— too many [doctors involved with animal testing]. I think for 5 lives, 10 lives, 15 human lives, we could save a million, 2 million, 10 million nonhuman lives."

A Campaign of Misinformation

To "sell" their story, animal extremists rely on the lack of public awareness of tight federal regulation on animal research— random inspections of facilities by the United States Department of Agriculture for compliance to the rigorous standards of the Animal Welfare Act.

Animal extremists wrongfully claim that data obtained from animal research cannot be extrapolated to drug development for humans. A recent survey of 150 drug compounds from twelve international pharmaceutical companies found that animal testing *had* significant predictive power to detect most—not all, admittedly—of 221 human toxic events caused by those drugs.

Animals are important not just in testing for efficacy and safety of drugs but also to the basic research that leads to medical advances. Ironically, animal extremists were decrying the uselessness of our center's basic investigations in primate stem cell biology on the very day in November 2007 that one of our scientists announced the first cloning of stem cells from non-embryonic primate tissue, subsequently hailed by *Time* magazine as the top discovery of 2007.

Animal extremists often show willful naïveté in considering human health needs. Smallpox, malaria, and polio have been nearly eradicated from much of the world—you no longer see wards of people confined to "iron lungs." Animal research is inextricably tied to improved human health. The first recognition of diabetes as a disease and the explanation of its cause, as well as its first treatment and early management, came directly from animal research conducted in universities. Improvements in treatments for this disease continue to come from these same sources. While these accomplishments are tributes to animal research, extremists fail to recognize that antibiotic-resistant tuberculosis, AIDS, diabetes, and heart disease still need the attention of researchers, who in turn need ethical animal research to advance their studies.

What are we to do when those very researchers are targeted for harassment and violence?

In 2006, members of ALF declared that they left a Molotov cocktail outside the Bel Air home of Dr. Lynn Fairbanks, the director of the Center for Primate Neuroethology at UCLA's [University of California at Los Angeles's] neuropsychiatric institute. Actually, the explosive device was placed on the porch of the faculty member's seventy-year-old neighbor. Fortunately, the timing device failed.

About one year later, a group calling themselves the Animal Liberation Brigade claimed responsibility for placing a lighted incendiary device next to a car parked at the home of Dr. Arthur Rosenbaum, who is chief of Pediatric Ophthalmology at UCLA's Jules Stein Eye Institute. Authorities described the event as "domestic terrorism." The delivery address was correct this time, but fortunately for Dr. Rosenbaum and his neighbors, the device did not ignite due to ineptness on the part of the "activists." Police noted that the device had the potential to create great harm.

Another talented researcher, Dr. Dario Ringach, ultimately gave in to animal extremists, promising to stop his research on monkeys in exchange for cessation of harassment of his family, including his young children. "You win," he e-mailed them.

It is worth mentioning that Ringach's, Rosenbaum's, and Fairbanks's research all were humanely conducted and met federal standards.

Medical Benefits of Animal Research for Animals and Humans

Vaccine Development

Humans

- Diphtheria
- Hepatitis
- Lyme Disease
- Measles
- Polio
- Rabies
- Rubella
- Tetanus
- Whooping Cough

Research

- AIDS
- Alzheimer's
- Blindness
- Cancer
- Diabetes
- Epilepsy
- Heart Disease
- Multiple Sclerosis
- New Drug Development
- Open Heart Surgery
- Spinal Cord Injury

- Allergies
- Birth Defects
- Burns
- Diarrhea in Infants
- Emphysema
- Glaucoma
- Huntingdon's Disease
- Muscular Dystrophy
- Nutrition
- Parkinson's Disease
- Tooth and Gum Disease

Treatment

- Allergies
- Anesthesia
- Antibiotics
- Artificial Joint Replacement
- Birth Defects
- Cancer
- Childhood Poisonings
- Diabetes
- Emphysema
- High Blood Pressure
- Kidney Disease
- Malaria
- Organ Transplants
- Stroke

continued

Medical Benefits of Animal Research for Animals and Humans [CONTINUED]

Vaccine Development	Research	Treatment
Animals	• Allergies	• Antibiotics
• Anthrax	• Artificial Insemination	• Artificial Joints for Dogs
• Blue Tongue in Sheep	• Improved Pain Killers	• Blood Transfusions
• Brucellosis in Cattle	• Embryo Transfer Techniques	• Cataracts
• Distemper in Dogs and Cats	• Inherited Diseases	• Glaucoma
• Equine Encephalitis	• Pet Food Nutrition	• Kidney Transplants
• Equine Rhino Virus	• Tooth and Gum Disease	• Lameness in Horses
• Equine Influenza		• Pet Cancer
• Feline Leukemia		• Orthopedic Surgery
• Hog Cholera		• Vitamin Deficiency
• Infectious Hepatitis Dogs		Diseases
• Lyme Disease		• Parasites
• Newcastle Disease in Poultry		–Giardiasis
• Parvo Virus in Dogs		–Heartworm
• Pneumonia Complex in Cats		–Hookworm
• Potomac Horse Fever		–External Parasites
• Rabies		–Leptospirosis
• Tetanus		

TAKEN FROM: P. Michael Conn and James V. Parker, "Warning: Animal Extremists are Dangerous to Your Health," *Skeptical Inquirer*, May–June 2008.

Far from Peaceful Protests

As you can see, we are not talking about peaceful protests here. As the editors of *Nature Neuroscience* put it, "Over several years, the researchers have been subjected to a campaign of harassment that included demonstrations at their homes and pamphlets distributed to their neighbors, as well as threatening phone calls and e-mails. Elsewhere, targets of similar protests have had abuse shouted through bullhorns or painted on their homes or cars, doorbells rung repeatedly, and windows smashed or doors broken down while family members were in the house. Animal rights Web sites post the names of scientists' spouses and children, along with their ages and schools."

According to the Foundation for Biomedical Research, a handful of illegal acts by animal extremist groups in 1994 had risen to a hundred such attacks ten years later. Society for Neuroscience members reported more attacks in the first six months of 2007 than in the five-year period from 1999 to 2003, prompting that organization to release, just this past February [2008], the document "Best Practices for Protecting Researchers and Research: Recommendations for Universities and Institutions."

Even though these and similar events send a chilling message to researchers and young people considering the field of biomedical research, they are poorly reported in the general media. The public doesn't hear about the impact this has on students viewing research as a potential career—or those already active in the field. Nor does it hear how the loss of talented researchers threatens creation of the new knowledge needed to devise cures.

Former University of Iowa president (now of Cornell University) David Skorton worries that researchers and students are being scared off by attacks from animal rights extremists. ALF, which took credit for break-ins and destruction at the University of Iowa, distributed the home addresses of researchers who conduct animal research to animal activists. "Publicizing this personal information was blatant intimidation," Skorton pointed out, adding that because of safety worries, "numerous researchers are even concerned about allowing their children to play in their own yards." He acknowledged that the cost of such intimidation is difficult to nail down, but he believed it "could be measured by many, many lives" that might not be saved by medical advances.

His words echoed those of Richard Bianco, vice president for research at the University of Minnesota, where an attack by vandals in 1999 caused more than $2 million in damage. "The financial aspect is the least of our problems. . . . The hardest thing is people see this and don't want to go into science," he said. "Why would they go into science when they can have their work threatened like that?"

Senator Orrin Hatch understood. "When research laboratories and university researchers are targeted and attacked, the ones who lose most are those who are living with a disease or who are watching a loved one struggling with a devastating illness."

Protecting the Victims of Terrorism

Because it seeks to stop ethical medical research, animal extremism is bad for our health. There are several steps the public can take to help reduce this threat to public health and good science.

We should be very careful in our giving to ensure that our contributions don't wind up aiding those who use the weapons of intimidation and violence. At the same time, we want to support organizations with proven records of caring for animals or of providing humane education that enhances the care received by laboratory animals.

If we have scientists who are neighbors, we can offer to organize a neighborhood watch and volunteer to speak to the media about how we have benefited from animal research if their homes are vandalized.

While mentioning the importance of speaking out, we can contact the local organization or university supporting research and offer to testify about what animal research has meant to someone in our family. When our kids come home from school with animal rights literature that denigrates animal research, we can contact their teachers to ask that they invite a researcher or veterinarian from a local university or research center to visit the class or even take the students on a tour of their facility.

It is because we thought it was time to sound the alarm that we wrote *The Animal Research War* describing what we think the public needs to know about this quiet war—"quiet," because it is seldom reported in the news. We want to tell people about the battle zone that we, as animal researchers, live in every day. We also want to communicate the benefits of animal research, past and potential, as well as the compassion with which researchers care for laboratory animals. If this war is lost, it is all who struggle with disease—that means all of us, sooner or later—who will bear the burden.

> *"Should we label violent animal rights extremists as terrorists? It makes sense to distinguish terrorist from violent extremist in order to maintain the right level of response to their acts."*

Extremist Animal Rights Activists Are Not Terrorists

Ben (Roger Panaman)

Ben is a pseudonym for Roger Panaman, a British zoologist with a particular interest in wolves. The following viewpoint is taken from his online book, How to Do Animal Rights—and Win the War on Animals. *In this excerpt, Ben discusses terrorism in general and explains why he thinks that violent animal rights activists should not be considered terrorists.*

As you read, consider the following questions:

1. Why does Ben say you should be careful when politicians and national bodies define terrorism?

2. Why does Ben say violent animal rights activists should not be considered terrorists?

3. Using the Boston Tea Party as an example, why does Ben say violent acts can be good for animals?

Terrorism is the systematic use by people of intimidation and violence, often against innocent people, to impel change in society. Through terrorism a small number of people can exert a disproportionate influence on society. Massive security forces are often ineffectual when combating a few dedicated terrorists who strike anywhere then vanish to fight another day.

Terrorist organisations are small, typically with around a dozen to a few hundred individuals, occasionally a few thousand. Violent animal rights extremists are often referred to as terrorists by some politicians and news media. Since the 1970s the number of violent animal rights extremists has been growing in Britain and their approach has spread abroad, especially to countries like Australia and the United States. However, despite the news reportage they stimulate, British violent animal rights extremists are thought to total only 300 to 400 people and draw on less active backing from 3,000 to 4,000 supporters.

Terrorism Is Not a New Concept

Terrorism is as old as history, but the expression terrorism originated in 18th-century revolutionary France. The state ordered the arrest, torture and execution of thousands of citizens during the French Revolution (1789), in the period known as the Reign of Terror, to murder political enemies and impose order on society. [Maximilien] Robespierre (1753–1794), French lawyer and radical political leader, is quoted as saying, "Terror is nothing but justice, prompt, severe and inflexible." Robespierre personally ordered dozens of executions and himself fell prey to the terror when he was imprisoned and guillotined.

Many people turned to terrorism after the Second World War when their nations sought independence from colonialism. Once they gained independence, however, several erstwhile terrorists became respected leaders of their country.

Menachem Begin (1913–1992) led the Irgun, a terrorist group fighting British rule in 1940s' Palestine. One of the Irgun's acts was bombing the King David Hotel in Jerusalem, the central British administrative offices, killing over 90 people. In 1977 Israel elected Begin as prime minister. Ironically, Israel then had to deal with Yasser Arafat (1929–2004), himself a one-time terrorist, fighting Israel for Palestinian independence, who subsequently became president of the Palestinian [National] Authority and a Nobel Prize winner for peace.

So terrorists do not necessarily remain contemptible shadowy figures, even though terrorism is rejected with horror and aversion by most people most of the time. A well-known phrase is 'someone's terrorist is someone else's freedom-fighter'; somebody is or is not a terrorist depending on where your political sympathies lie. You can always justify your terrorist inclinations by appealing to philosophy. With a utilitarian attitude your doctrine would be *better that a few people should die if necessary for the majority of people.* Under a deontology viewpoint your doctrine would be *you must do your duty irrespective of the consequences, be they good or bad.*

Definitions of Terrorism May Be Political

Terrorism causes widespread public anxiety because anyone may be injured or killed. But for national governments to fight terrorism effectively they first need to know what they are fighting. Exactly what terrorism is, however, and who is and who is not a terrorist, have always eluded clear definition. What happens in actuality is that both sides in a dispute often convincingly employ words like *terrorism* and *terrorist* to bring discredit on the opposing side.

So you must be careful when politicians and national bodies define terrorism. Who are these politicians and national bodies, what are their political interests and how exactly do they propose to tackle terrorism? If you are not careful they may fool and manipulate you into furthering their questionable political aims. You may find yourself sanctioning laws and actions that buttress their powers but conflict with democratic society and work against your personal liberty.

Violent Animal Rights Extremists Are Not Terrorists

Politicians, the news media, and people with vested interests in animals sometimes accuse animal rights extremists of terrorism. Violent animal rights extremism is largely confined to Europe and North America and began in Britain in the mid-1970s where extremists began using violent methods to make their point or intimidate people, such as livestock exporters, fur traders, animal breeders and animal laboratory workers.

It is fair to say that these activities should not be taken lightly. Some of them, like arson, carry a jail sentence and others, like setting up letter bombs and booby traps, can cause serious injury. However, although there have been narrow escapes, violent animal rights extremists have not intentionally killed anyone with such conduct. On the other hand some animal rights activists have died while on actions.

Should we label violent animal rights extremists as terrorists? It makes sense to distinguish terrorist from violent extremist in order to maintain the right level of response to their acts. Terrorists, like the Irgun and today's al Qaeda, do not hesitate to kill people deliberately. Al Qaeda terrorists hijacked four airliners in the US and using them as guided missiles killed 3,000 innocent people in 2001. It would be an overreaction, but one often found in the news media, to lump violent animal rights extremists with terrorists.

Direct Actions Sometimes Lead to Big Effects

No one can say with certainty whether direct action or extremism for any cause is efficacious. Discussing animal rights, [animal rights advocate] Richard Ryder sums it up:

The Number of Animals Used in Research, FY 2005–2007

Fiscal Year (FY)	Dogs	Cats	Primates	Guinea Pigs	Hamsters	Rabbits	Farm Animals	Other Covered Animals	Totals
2005	66,610	22,921	57,531	221,286	176,988	245,786	155,004	231,440	1,177,566
2006	66,314	21,637	62,315	204,809	167,571	239,720	105,780	144,567	1,012,713
2007	72,037	22,687	69,990	207,257	172,498	236,511	109,961	136,509	1,027,450

TAKEN FROM: U.S. Department of Agriculture, Animal and Plant Health Inspection Service, Animal Care Annual Report of Activities, Fiscal Year 2007. Appendix 5. www.aphis.usda.gov.

Yet any historian knows that in some earlier reform movements little progress was made until illegal and sometimes violent acts occurred. Whether reforms would have been achieved without the direct action of the suffragists, for example, or whether they would have been achieved more slowly, are matters for conjecture.

Most people might agree that extreme actions can sometimes lead to big effects. The Boston Tea Party is an often cited case. Angered at having to pay taxes to the British crown without parliamentary representation, colonialists in Massachusetts in 1773 flung the consignment of tea, on which tax had to be paid, off merchant ships into Boston Harbour. Their act developed into the American War of Independence, radically changed American society and led in 1776 to the world's first major declaration of human rights.

One ingredient of the Boston Tea Party that led to the American War of Independence was the publicity the action created. People delight in reading about excessive and exceptional human behaviour—and the modern news media deluge us with extremisms. Violence gets noticed; quiet initiatives are seldom trumpeted. Whether publicity caused by animal rights extremism is good or bad, there is no doubt that it thrusts animal rights into the public conscience. Extreme direct action stirs up controversy, stimulates debate and keeps it alive; when it comes to animal rights you might therefore argue that extremism is good for animals (i.e., it gets publicity).

The flip side of extreme action is quietly and politely improving attitudes by education and argument, by appealing to rationality, compassion and a sense of justice, and by changes in the law. This is slow work but effective in that it makes for a great and long-lasting change in people's attitudes and in most wars it is attitudes that must be won.

It is impossible to know the single best way to bring about a revolution in society. The most sensible means is probably to advance on a broad front, everyone doing the best they can in their own way.

> *"This was not the act of a lone extremist. It is one more act of violence to add to a long, long list of crimes committed by anti-choice terrorists."*

Extremist Pro-Life Groups Are Responsible for the Murder of George Tiller

Jill Filipovic

On May 31, 2009, George Tiller was shot to death while attending a service at Reformation Lutheran Church in Wichita, Kansas. Tiller was one of three medical doctors in the United States who performed abortions after the twenty-first week of pregnancy (late-term abortions). Operation Rescue, a pro-life group, conducted protests against Tiller for many years. The following viewpoint, written by New York-based journalist Jill Filipovic, was published by the Guardian *the day after Tiller was killed. Filipovic contends that the pro-life group shares responsibility for Tiller's murder, along with the actual shooter, because the organization's beliefs influenced his actions.*

As you read, consider the following questions:

1. According to Filipovic, how many people in the United States have been murdered by anti-choice terrorists?

2. Why does Filipovic say pro-life organizations can't be surprised when their followers kill doctors?

3. What does Filipovic mean when she says "words mean things"?

George Tiller, a Kansas physician, was shot to death in church on Sunday [May 31, 2009]. He was one of only a handful of doctors in the United States providing late-term therapeutic abortions for women in need—women whose pregnancies threatened their lives or their health, and women who learned that they were carrying foetuses with severe abnormalities. Women travelled across the country to see Tiller when their own physicians and local medical providers couldn't help them. For many women, Tiller was, as one of his patients put it, "the one shining light in the worst week of my life".

He was also a major lightning rod in the abortion wars. Anti-choicers harassed his patients, day in and day out. They bombed his clinic. They shot him once before. They filed lawsuit after lawsuit and even convinced local prosecutors to launch criminal investigations and trials (none were successful). They published his home address and the full names of his family members on their Web sites. They posted information about anyone who did business with him, from where he got his coffee to where he did his dry cleaning.

They had him and his staff wearing bullet-proof vests to work every day. Tiller drove an armoured car and protected his home with a state-of-the-art security system. And, to better enable stalking and harassment, they posted his daily comings and goings—including the fact that he attended services every Sunday at Reformation Lutheran Church, the place where he was ultimately shot and killed.

All because he was a licensed physician who performed legal medical procedures.

Tiller's Killer Is Affiliated with the Pro-Life Movement

Not surprisingly, his killer is strongly suspected to be affiliated with the "pro-life" movement. If that's the case, it makes Tiller the 10th person in the United States to be murdered by anti-choice terrorists.

And that's just the tip of the iceberg. Since 1977, there have been at least 17 attempted murders, 383 death threats, 153 incidents of assault or battery and three kidnappings committed against abortion providers in North America. Tiller himself survived an assassination attempt in 1993.

Some pro-life groups are issuing statements of condemnation and attempting to paint this murder as the work of an extremist. But this latest act of terrorism is, sadly, not an anomaly. It is part of a clearly established pattern of harassment, intimidation and violence against abortion providers and pro-choice individuals. And mainstream pro-life groups shoulder much of the blame.

Pro-life organisations routinely refer to abortion as "murder", a "genocide" and a "holocaust". They post the full names [of] abortion providers on their Web sites, along with their addresses, their license plate numbers, their photos, the names of children and the schools those children attend (sometimes with helpful Wild-West-style "Wanted" posters offering $5,000 rewards).

When you convince your followers that abortion providers are the equivalent of SS [Nazi] officers slaughtering innocents by the millions, tell them that "it's all-out WAR" against pro-choicers and then provide the home addresses and personal information of the "monster" "late-term baby killer" abortion providers you're supposedly at war against, you can't act sur-

Incidents of Violence and Disruption Against Abortion Providers in the U.S. and Canada

Violence	1977–93	1994	1995	1996	1997	1998
Murder	1	4	0	0	0	2
Attempted Murder	3	8	1	1	2	1
Bombing	28	1	1	2	6	1
Arson	113	11	14	3	8	4
Attempted Bomb/ Arson	61	3	1	4	2	5
Invasion	345	2	4	0	7	5
Vandalism	543	42	31	29	105	46
Trespassing	0	0	0	0	0	0
Butyric Acid Attacks	72	8	0	1	0	19
Anthrax Threats	0	0	0	0	0	12
Assault & Battery	88	7	2	1	9	4
Death Threats	166	59	41	13	11	25
Kidnapping	2	0	0	0	0	1
Burglary	31	3	3	6	6	6
Stalking	188	22	61	52	67	13
Total	1,641	170	159	112	223	144
Disruption						
Hate Mail/ Harassing Calls	1,452	381	255	605	2,829	915
Email/Internet Harassment	0	0	0	0	0	0
Hoax Device/ Susp. Package	0	0	0	0	0	0
Bomb Threats	297	14	41	13	79	31
Picketing	6,361	1,407	1,356	3,932	7,518	8,402
Total	8,110	1,802	1,652	4,550	10,426	9,348
Clinic Blockades						
Number of Incidents	609	25	5	7	25	2
Number of Arrests	33,444	217	54	65	29	16

continued

prised when those followers conclude that it's morally justified to use the information to kill doctors.

Incidents of Violence and Disruption Against Abortion Providers in the U.S. and Canada [CONTINUED]

Violence	1999	2000	2001	2002	2003	2004
Murder	0	0	0	0	0	0
Attempted Murder	0	1	0	0	0	0
Bombing	1	0	1	0	0	0
Arson	8	2	2	1	3	2
Attempted Bomb/ Arson	1	3	2	0	0	1
Invasion	3	4	2	1	0	0
Vandalism	63	56	58	60	48	49
Trespassing	193	81	144	163	66	67
Butyric Acid Attacks	0	0	0	0	0	0
Anthrax Threats	35	30	554	23	0	1
Assault & Battery	2	7	2	1	7	8
Death Threats	13	9	14	3	7	4
Kidnapping	0	0	0	0	0	0
Burglary	4	5	6	1	9	5
Stalking	13	17	10	12	3	15
Total	336	215	795	265	143	152
Disruption						
Hate Mail/ Harassing Calls	1,646	1,011	404	230	432	453
Email/Internet Harassment	0	0	0	24	70	51
Hoax Device/ Susp. Package	0	0	0	41	13	9
Bomb Threats	39	20	31	7	17	13
Picketing	8,727	8,478	9,969	10,241	11,348	11,640
Total	10,412	9,509	10,404	10,543	11,880	12,166
Clinic Blockades						
Number of Incidents	3	4	2	4	10	34
Number of Arrests	5	0	0	0	0	0

continued

Incidents of Violence and Disruption Against Abortion Providers in the U.S. and Canada [CONTINUED]

Violence	2005	2006	2007	2008	2009	Total
Murder	0	0	0	0	1	8
Attempted Murder	0	0	0	0	0	17
Bombing	0	0	0	0	0	41
Arson	2	0	2	0	0	175
Attempted Bomb/ Arson	6	4	2	1	0	96
Invasion	0	4	7	6	0	390
Vandalism	83	72	59	45	11	1,400
Trespassing	633	336	122	148	40	1,993
Butyric Acid Attacks	0	0	0	0	0	100
Anthrax Threats	0	0	1	3	0	659
Assault & Battery	8	11	12	6	4	179
Death Threats	10	10	13	2	6	406
Kidnapping	0	1	0	0	0	4
Burglary	11	30	12	7	6	151
Stalking	8	6	19	19	0	525
Total	761	474	249	237	67	6,143
Disruption						
Hate Mail/ Harassing Calls	515	548	522	396	1,401	13,995
Email/Internet Harassment	77	25	38	44	10	339
Hoax Device/ Susp. Package	16	17	23	24	5	148
Bomb Threats	11	7	6	13	3	642
Picketing	13,415	13,505	11,113	12,503	1,922	141,837
Total	14,034	14,102	11,702	12,980	3,341	156,961
Clinic Blockades						
Number of Incidents	4	13	7	8	1	763
Number of Arrests	0	0	3	1	0	33,834

TAKEN FROM: "NAF Violence and Disruption Statistics," National Abortion Federation, 2009. www.prochoice.org.

Mainstream Pro-Lifers Applauded Tiller's Murder

These are not fringe groups. Conservative television personality Bill O'Reilly called Tiller's clinic a "death mill", referred to Tiller as a "baby killer" who was "executing babies about to be born" and said Tiller was doing "Nazi stuff" for which he "had blood on his hands".

Frank Pavone, a Roman Catholic priest, member of James Dobson's Focus on the Family and director of Priests for Life, posted a YouTube video on Sunday to say that he "abhors" the violence committed against Tiller but "we just don't know and we shouldn't jump to conclusions" in assuming that an antichoice terrorist may have murdered Tiller—although, he concedes, someone may have assassinated him "in order to stop Tiller from killing more babies". He continued: "When we talk about abortion, we are talking about killing. There's no two ways about it. . . . This is a massive holocaust, it is killing."

Pavone is chummy with Operation Rescue founder Randall Terry, who had this to say about Tiller's assassination:

> George Tiller was a mass-murderer. We grieve for him that he did not have time to properly prepare his soul to face God. I am more concerned that the [President Barack] Obama administration will use Tiller's killing to intimidate pro-lifers into surrendering our most effective rhetoric and actions. Abortion is still murder. And we still must call abortion by its proper name: murder.

> Those men and women who slaughter the unborn are murderers according to the law of God. We must continue to expose them in our communities and peacefully protest them at their offices and homes, and yes, even their churches.

That's some definition of "peacefully protesting".

The prime suspect in Tiller's murder appears to have frequented the Operation Rescue Web site (which had its own "Tiller Watch" section), and took part in some of those "peaceful protests" that anti-choicers hold so dear. Far from a random extremist, he appears to have been fairly entrenched in the anti-choice movement.

And if he is the person who murdered Tiller, he isn't alone among pro-lifers who embrace Terry's directive that, "If you think abortion is murder, act like it." (After all, Terry has posited, "Wouldn't it have been OK to kill Hitler if you knew you could save millions of Jews?").

Self-identified pro-lifers have celebrated Tiller's murder, leaving hundreds of comments on right-wing blogs (and a good number at progressive and pro-choice blogs, just for good measure). Conservative writer LaShawn Barber gloated at the "irony" of "Tiller the child killer, cultivator of death" being murdered at church. A quick perusal of the front page of ProLifeBlogs.com includes such headlines as "George Tiller has killed his last baby," "Baby killer Tiller shot, killed at church," "Tiller the Killer killed," "Today Tiller the Killer, now a martyr for Molech, met God" and "Tiller shot to death!"

These are not "bad apples". They are symptomatic of (and sometimes the spokespeople for) a larger movement that is disturbed and dangerous.

Mainstream Pro-Life Groups Do Not Care About Life

While individuals who self-identify as pro-life may be well-meaning and against violence, mainstream pro-life groups and the people who run them do not care about life, before or after birth. And while today anti-choice groups are halfheartedly condemning Tiller's murder, they continue to use the same outlandish and inflammatory rhetoric that inspired and enabled it.

Words mean things. Anti-choicers should certainly have every right to express their views, but they must also realise that actions have consequences and their rhetoric is not harmless. If you yell "Fire!" in a crowded theatre, it's reasonably foreseeable that people will panic and someone will be injured. And if you yell "Murderer!" "Baby Killer!" and "Holocaust!" long enough, it's reasonably foreseeable that someone will take it upon themselves to make sure that vigilante justice is done (especially if you provide the name and address of the person who you claim is committing "genocide").

This was not the act of a lone extremist. It is one more act of violence to add to a long, long list of crimes committed by anti-choice terrorists, and it is the logical outcome of years of increasingly violent, dehumanising and threatening rhetoric and action on the part of supposedly mainstream pro-life groups. The responsibility for George Tiller's death surely falls on the shoulders of the person who actually pulled the trigger. But when pro-life groups did everything but give him a gun, their hands are hardly clean.

| "The Christian Right's responsible re-
action to the death of George Tiller
should put to rest the lie that Judeo-
Christian extremists are anywhere near
as numerous or dangerous as those of
the Muslim variety."

Extremist Pro-Life Groups Are Not Responsible for the Murder of George Tiller

James Kirchick

*On May 31, 2009, George Tiller was shot to death while attend-
ing a service at Reformation Lutheran Church in Wichita, Kansas. Tiller was one of three medical doctors in the United States
who performed abortions after the twenty-first week of pregnancy (late-term abortions). Operation Rescue, a pro-life group,
conducted protests against Tiller for many years. The following
viewpoint by James Kirchick, a writer for the* New Republic *and
the* Advocate, *contends that pro-life groups should not be held
responsible for Tiller's murder. He argues that antiabortion*

James Kirchick, "The Religious Right Didn't Kill George Tiller," *Wall Street Journal*,
June 3, 2009, p. A17. Copyright © 2009 Dow Jones & Company, Inc. All rights
reserved. Reprinted with permission of The Wall Street Journal and the author.

groups made statements denouncing the attack and they should not be compared with Islamic extremist groups who compete to claim responsibility when a suicide bomb goes off.

As you read, consider the following questions:

1. How does Kirchick say Operation Rescue responded to Tiller's murder?
2. According to Kirchick, what does liberal Stephen Pizzo say about the fundamental Christians?
3. How does Kirchick say "Christianists" would react to the murder if they were actual religious fascists?

On Sunday [May 31, 2009], abortion doctor George Tiller was murdered at his church in Wichita, Kan. He was one of a handful of doctors in the U.S. who performed late-term abortions and for decades had been a target of virulent criticism from antiabortion activists. His clinic had been bombed and vandalized, and in 1993, he was shot in both arms in a failed assassination attempt. Tiller's alleged killer, Scott Roeder, is a long-time radical antiabortion activist with reported ties to a militant antigovernment organization called the [Montana] Freemen.

Within hours after the murder, every antiabortion group in the country denounced the attack. Robert P. George, a leading Catholic intellectual opponent of abortion, wrote that "George Tiller's life was precious" and characterized his murder as "a gravely wicked thing." He called on his fellow abortion opponents to "teach that violence against abortionists is not the answer to the violence of abortion."

Even Operation Rescue, the extreme antiabortion group that organized a six-week blockade of Tiller's office in 1991, issued a statement condemning the murder. "We denounce vigilantism and the cowardly act that took place this morning," Troy Newman, the organization's president, said.

The Organized Antiabortion Movement Opposes Violence

These unqualified reproaches are nothing new. The organized antiabortion movement has always opposed violence against abortion providers. That has never stopped opportunistic prochoice activists, however, from conflating their passionate rhetoric with the behavior of individual criminals. True to form, on Sunday, Mike Hendricks of the *Kansas City Star* accused anyone who had criticized Tiller as a murderer (Tiller aborted healthy, nine-month old fetuses) of being an "accomplice" to his death.

Over the past decade this argumentative tactic has taken on an even more insidious twist. In addition to fighting violent, Muslim jihadists ["holy warriors"] abroad, some liberals argue that America must deal with its own, homegrown terrorists. These are not just people who commit violence but millions of socially conservative evangelicals and Catholics—"Christianists"—who comprise the base of the Republican Party and threaten the stability of the country.

In 2007, former *New York Times* Middle East Bureau Chief Chris Hedges published a book called *American Fascists* that compared conservative evangelicals to European brownshirts [Nazis] of the 1920s and 1930s. That same year, CNN's Christiane Amanpour hosted a three-part series, *God's Warriors*, that equated Christian (and Jewish) fundamentalists with Muslim extremists.

The Religious Right Should Not Be Compared to Islamic Extremists

The comparison between the religious Right and Islamic extremists is invariably partisan so as to smear the GOP [Republican Party] as being held hostage to forces as dangerous as Hamas or Hezbollah. "Even as the [George W.] Bush ad-

Americans Hold a Variety of Views About Abortion

U.S. Religious Traditions	Legal in all cases	Legal in most cases	Illegal in most cases	Illegal in all cases	Don't know/ refused	Sample Size
National Total:	18%	33%	27%	16%	6%	35,556
Evangelical Churches	9%	24%	36%	25%	6%	9,472
Mainline Churches	20%	42%	25%	7%	7%	7,470
Historically Black Churches	18%	29%	23%	23%	8%	1,995
Catholics	16%	32%	27%	18%	7%	8,054
Mormons	8%	19%	61%	9%	4%	581
Orthodox	24%	38%	20%	10%	8%	363
Jehovah's Witnesses	5%	11%	25%	52%	7%	215
Other Christians	33%	42%	13%	6%	7%	129
Jews	40%	44%	9%	5%	2%	682
Muslims	13%	35%	35%	13%	4%	116
Buddhists	35%	46%	10%	3%	6%	411
Hindus	23%	46%	19%	5%	7%	257
Other Faiths	36%	41%	13%	4%	6%	449
Unaffiliated	29%	41%	16%	8%	6%	5,048

TAKEN FROM: U.S. Religious Landscape Survey.

ministration denounces and battles Islamic religious zealotry abroad, fundamental Christian zealotry is taking hold here at home," wrote Stephen Pizzo on the liberal AlterNet Web site in 2004. On his popular HBO program, comedian Bill Maher frequently compares murderous Islamists to censorious Christians.

But if the reactions to the death of Tiller mean anything, the "Christian Taliban," as conservative religious figures are often called, isn't living up to its namesake. If "Christianists" were anything like actual religious fascists they would applaud Tiller's murder as a "heroic martyrdom operation" and suborn further mayhem.

Radical Islamists revel in death. Just witness the videos that suicide bombers record before they carry out their murderous task or listen to the homicidal exhortations of extremist imams [religious leaders]. Murder—particularly of the unarmed and innocent—is a righteous deed for these people. The manifestos of Islamic militant groups are replete with paeans to killing infidels. When a suicide bomb goes off in Israel, Palestinian terrorist factions compete to claim responsibility for the carnage.

There is no appreciable number of people in this country, religious Christians or otherwise, who support the murder of abortion doctors. The same cannot be said of Muslims who support suicide bombings in the name of their religion.

Yet speak of the disproportionately violent strain in Islam to a "progressive" person and you'll be met with sneering recitations of millennia-old Christian crusades or Jewish settlements in the West Bank. As for conservative Christians' contemporary political endeavors, lobbying to ban the teaching of evolution in schools or forbidding same-sex marriage simply does not threaten society in quite the same way as the genital mutilation of young girls or the bombing of the London transit system.

I happen to support a legal regime that would, in Bill Clinton's famous words, keep abortion safe, legal and rare. I hold no brief for the religious Right, and its views on homosexuality in particular offend (and affect) me personally. But it's precisely because of my identity that I consider comparisons between so-called Christianists (who seek to limit my rights via the ballot box) and Islamic fundamentalists (who seek to limit my rights via decapitation) to be fatuous.

The Christian Right Reacted Responsibly

In the coming days, we will hear more about how mainstream conservative organizations and media personalities created an "environment" in which the murder of an abortion doctor became an inevitability. Just as talk radio was blamed for the 1995 Oklahoma City bombing, an attempt will be made to extend the guilt for this crime from the individual who pulled the trigger to the conservative movement writ large. But the Christian Right's responsible reaction to the death of George Tiller should put to rest the lie that Judeo-Christian extremists are anywhere near as numerous or dangerous as those of the Muslim variety.

> *"What distinguishes pro-life bombers and assassins is not the degree of their moral conviction, but their fanatical commitment to a certain understanding of political theology."*

Pro-Life Extremists Are Characterized by a Fanatical Commitment

Jon A. Shields

Jon A. Shields is a professor of government at Claremont McKenna College. In the following viewpoint, he takes a historical look at the pro-life movement, paying specific attention to the change from peaceful civil disobedience to bombing empty abortion clinics to outright killing of doctors who perform abortions. He particularly considers the theology behind their actions, which he believes is behind their violent behaviors.

As you read, consider the following questions:

1. How does Shields say Randall Terry sold the idea of Operation Rescue to Protestants who had not previously been involved in the abortion conflict?

2. What theology from John Knox convinced Michael Bray to bomb abortion clinics?

3. What was the stated purpose of the Army of God?

The recent [May 31, 2009] murder of late-term abortion specialist Dr. George Tiller cast a spotlight once again on the violent fringe of the pro-life movement. What motivates them? How do they differ from the law-abiding citizens who work and demonstrate against abortion?

Some critics of the pro-life movement have recycled the old charge that what sets the handful of violent pro-lifers apart is their moral seriousness. Unlike the hypocrites who content themselves with protests and lobbying, the argument goes, those who bomb clinics and assassinate abortionists have the courage of their conviction that abortion is murder. Writes William Saletan in *Slate*, "If a doctor in Kansas were butchering hundreds of old or disabled people, I doubt most members of the National Right to Life Committee would stand by. Somebody would use force." The fringe who kill expose the mainstream of pro-lifers as frauds.

Pro-Life Extremists Are Committed to a Certain Political Theology

The reality is much more interesting. The best studies of pro-life extremism—notably James Risen and Judy L. Thomas's *Wrath of Angels*—make clear that what distinguishes pro-life bombers and assassins is not the degree of their moral conviction, but their fanatical commitment to a certain understanding of political theology.

When abortion emerged as a public issue in the 1960s, most of those who fought to keep the practice illegal were Catholics. Most Protestants, including virtually all evangelicals, stayed on the sidelines. The Southern Baptist Convention even tacitly blessed *Roe v. Wade*, the 1973 decision by which the Supreme Court held abortion to be an individual right, overturning the laws of 50 states.

Roe divided the pro-lifers. Most continued to work through political channels, joining state affiliates of the National Right to Life Committee. But some concluded that either amending the Constitution or transforming the composition of the Supreme Court might not be achievable in their lifetime. In frustration, they began a campaign of sit-ins. Thus, *Roe* energized pro-lifers, pushing many activists into the streets.

Early Pro-Lifers Practiced Nonviolence

From the beginning, their civil disobedience was shaped by their theology. The early Catholic activists came out of the antiwar Left and were inspired by liberal Christians. John O'Keefe, the founder of the rescue movement (whose name derives from Proverbs 24:11: "Rescue those being led away to death; hold back those staggering toward slaughter"), was deeply influenced by Martin Luther King Jr. and especially the Catholic monk Thomas Merton. O'Keefe wrote a recruiting pamphlet, *A Peaceful Presence* (1978), that encouraged pro-lifers to practice nonviolent civil disobedience (blocking clinic entrances, for example, and going limp when arrested) as a spiritual act and a symbolic sharing in the helplessness of unborn children.

Early rescuers asked their friends in the antiwar movement and other liberal causes to join them but were roundly rebuffed. Yet even as those pleas fell on deaf ears, conservative evangelicals were rethinking their own political theology in ways that would forever change the rescue movement.

Given the recent history of the evangelical Right, it is easy to forget just how apolitical large numbers of conservative Protestants were during most of the 20th century. Evangelicals, in particular, tended to believe that saving souls by spreading the gospel should take priority over political engagement. Most also accepted a view of the end times known as premillennialism, which teaches that the world must fall even deeper into sin before Christ returns to establish his thousand-year reign. This eschatological view encouraged separation from the world and made social reform seem futile at best.

By the late sixties liberals were criticizing evangelicals for neglecting the great public questions of the day. The conservative Presbyterian Francis Schaeffer agreed. More than any other thinker, Schaeffer mobilized evangelicals to join the pro-life movement by changing the way they thought about politics. Contrary to the prevailing emphasis in evangelical churches, Schaeffer insisted that Christians had a duty to make the world better rather than barricade themselves in subcultures. He further taught that political quietism did not follow from premillennialism. As he put it, "Even if I knew the world was going to end tomorrow, I would still plant a tree today."

Schaeffer advocated defiance of government in the matter of abortion. In *A Christian Manifesto* (1981), he concluded, "At a certain point there is not only the right, but the duty, to disobey the state." This was heady stuff for a subculture that had long insisted that any social movement was a distraction from the Great Commission, Jesus' command to his followers to "go and make disciples of all nations."

Operation Rescue Was More Militant than Early Pro-Life Groups

Nearly every evangelical leader who became prominent in the pro-life movement credited Schaeffer for clearing away the theological obstacles to activism. Among them was Randall Terry, an evangelical convert who turned the rescue movement into something big.

Terry succeeded where O'Keefe had failed. He founded Operation Rescue in 1986 and built it into the largest campaign of civil disobedience since the anti-Vietnam war movement, engineering massive blockades of abortion clinics in New York, Atlanta, Los Angeles, and Wichita. The National

Abortion Federation estimates that between 1977 and 1993, the movement was responsible for more than 600 blockades leading to over 33,000 arrests.

The success of Operation Rescue turned on the power of particular religious appeals. Terry approached independent fundamentalist pastors and told them that evangelicals had blood on their hands because they had stayed out of the abortion conflict. Critics who disparaged the rescue movement as self-righteous misunderstood it: It was a way for evangelicals to show repentance for their sins. As Risen and Thomas explain, "Terry would sell the church on Operation Rescue as a form of atonement."

The fundamentalists in Operation Rescue did tend to be more militant than the early Catholic demonstrators. Rather than simply go limp and let police officers arrest them, for instance, many resisted by grabbing onto whatever they could. Nonetheless, they were far from violent. (Many, in fact, complained of police brutality.) Not all participants, however, were persuaded by Schaeffer's insistence that their agitation be peaceful. A handful radicalized his teachings to justify and inspire violence.

Clinic Bombings Were First Orchestrated by Michael Bray

There is little in Michael Bray's early life to suggest that he would become the spiritual leader of the violent fringe. At Bowie High School in Maryland, he was a football player and state wrestling champion. He was an Eagle Scout. Following in his father's footsteps, he earned a spot at the U.S. Naval Academy.

But Bray dropped out of the academy and hitchhiked across the country seeking adventure and direction. In Orlando he attended a Baptist tent revival and began thinking seriously about a life of faith. His search for God included flirtations with Mormonism and the Conservative Baptist Association [of America]. Under the influence of Schaeffer's writings, however, Bray was drawn to major figures of the Protestant Reformation of the 16th century, especially John Calvin and John Knox.

Calvin emphasized the biblical doctrine of predestination, that God determined who would be saved and damned before the creation of the world. Not only are the "elect" chosen by God for salvation, but, according to Calvin, they should also govern. Only public officials, however, could legitimately use force to punish crimes.

Knox disagreed. He suggested that any member of the elect, not just public officials, could use force to achieve God's justice. As Risen and Thomas underscore, Knox's teachings convinced Bray that "it was appropriate for the godly man to take the law into his own hands, because his hands were the tools of the Lord." Indeed, Bray actually "came to believe John Knox was speaking to him across the centuries, telling him that it was his duty as a Christian to fight abortion by any means necessary."

Bray soon began orchestrating clinic bombings, for which he would serve time in prison. In 1984 he and his impressionable protégés Michael Spinks and Kenneth Shields (no relation to the author) helped set an annual record for bombings that stands to this day. Abortion facilities were bombed in six cities in the Washington, D.C., region. These early attacks, however, were successfully timed to avoid human casualties.

Abortion Providers Were Targeted for Execution

In the early 1990s, Operation Rescue collapsed under the weight of its participants' exhaustion and Terry's authoritarian leadership. Then in 1994, a new federal law increased the penalties for blocking access to clinics. Now isolated, the seriously violence-prone were left to their own worst impulses. Violence escalated. For the first time, abortion providers were targeted for execution. In the period 1993–98, six people were killed by four shooters, and a seventh lost his life in a clinic bombing.

The extremists coalesced in what they called the Army of God and declared war: "We, the remnant of God-fearing men and women of the United States of Amerika, do officially declare war on the entire child-killing industry." Army of God manuals contained instructions on how to acquire explosives and bomb clinics.

For inspiration, the radicals turned to Bray's *A Time to Kill* (1994), a book that could not have been more different from O'Keefe's *A Peaceful Presence*. As Risen and Thomas report, Bray became the "national spokesperson for violence and retribution" and his book "must reading among extremists."

One of these was Paul Hill, a radical Presbyterian minister, a graduate of the Reformed Theological Seminary, who quickly rose to leadership in the Army of God. He was the author of the group's infamous 1994 "Defensive Action Statement," a petition endorsing violence that was signed by 29 radicals. Hill would be executed by the state of Florida in 2003 for killing an abortion doctor and a clinic escort.

Shelley Shannon also found inspiration in Bray's writings. A housewife, Shannon bombed clinics in four states before wounding George Tiller in an attempt on his life in 1993. She is now in prison. In her diary, Shannon described her religious experiences just prior to various acts of violence. Hours before she bombed a clinic, for instance, she wrote: "If I die doing this, I die in Christ, walking obediently in a work He gave me." And hours before shooting Tiller, she reflected, "This morning in bed it seemed God asked, Is there any doubt?" "No, Lord. Please help me do it right."

Others, whether or not they were directly influenced by Bray's writings, shared his disregard for the legitimacy and authority of the American government. Scott Roeder, who has been charged with Tiller's murder, is a member of the Montana Freemen, a Christian organization that has declared itself outside the authority of the government and engaged in an armed conflict with the FBI [Federal Bureau of Investigation] in 1996.

Most Violent Pro-Lifers Quote a Handful of Scriptures

Whatever the shades of difference among them, virtually all the radicals have cherished a bellicose reading of a handful of Old Testament verses, especially Genesis 9:6: "Whoever sheds the blood of man, by man shall his blood be shed; for in the image of God has God made man." The fringe seemingly ignore the New Testament, particularly the passages enjoining respect for civil authorities.

In the aftermath of Tiller's shooting, pro-life organizations were quick to denounce vigilante justice and reaffirm their well-established fidelity to American democracy. As post-1960s activism goes, the pro-life movement is unusually patriotic. Its many Catholic and Protestant participants, moreover, obviously do not understand their faith to require them to kill doctors or nurses—or mothers or fathers—involved in the great evil of abortion. On the contrary, their behavior is generally consonant with orthodox Christian teaching on murder ("Thou shalt not.") civil government ("Render unto Caesar"), and the duty of believers to do good and resist evil by all legitimate means.

Periodical Bibliography

The following articles have been selected to supplement the diverse views presented in this chapter.

Michael Conn and James Parker	"Winners and Losers in the Animal Research Wars," *American Scientist*, May–June 2008.
Mary Eberstadt	"Pro-Animal, Pro-Life," *First Things*, June–July 2009.
Bonnie Erbe	"Tiller Murder Is Terrorism, and All Pro-Life Extremists Are to Blame," *U.S. News & World Report Online*, June 1, 2009. http://politics.usnews.com.
Holly Fletcher	"Militant Extremists in the United States," Council on Foreign Relations, April 21, 2008. www.cfr.org.
Brady Huggett	"When Animal Rights Turns Ugly," *Nature Biotechnology*, June 2008.
Dara Lovitz	"Animal Lovers and Tree Huggers Are the New Cold-Blooded Criminals? Examining the Flaws of Ecoterrorism Bills," *Journal of Animal Law*, 2007.
Carol Mason	"The Hillbilly Defense: Culturally Mediating U.S. Terror at Home and Abroad," *NWSA Journal*, Fall 2005.
Terry O'Neill	"Animal Rights and the Culture of Death," *Catholic Insight*, November 1, 2008.
Jesse Walker	"Protect & Serve: The Oath Keepers Have More in Common with Henry David Thoreau than Timothy McVeigh," *American Conservative*, May 1, 2010.
Barbara Young	"Battling Anti-Meat Terrorists," *National Provisioner*, December 1, 2008.

For Further Discussion

Chapter 1

1. Jan G. Linn contends that members of the Christian Right are extremist because they behave as if they alone know and do the will of God. Sarah Pulliam objects to the term "Religious Right" because she does not believe that evangelical Christians are extremists. Do you think Christians with conservative or evangelical beliefs are necessarily extremists? Is it possible that some are extremists while others are not? Use the viewpoints in this chapter to support your views.

Chapter 2

1. This chapter presents several perspectives on what motivates Islamic extremists. What factor or factors do you think are the most important causes of Islamic extremism? Why?

2. Bill Musk says that killing the enemy is a necessary part of Islamic jihad. After reading the viewpoint in this chapter, what do you think?

Chapter 3

1. The viewpoints in this chapter present a number of perspectives on ways that extremism might be countered. Do you think it is possible to counter extremism? If so, how? If not, why not? Use the viewpoints in this chapter to support your answers.

2. Samir Khalil Samir says that terrorism is taught in Islamic schools. Jay Tolson says that Islamic schools can be part of the solution to terrorism rather than part of the problem. Do you think that Islamic schools should be allowed in

non-Muslim countries? Can Islamic schools help to counter terrorism?

Chapter 4

1. According to P. Michael Conn and James V. Parker, animal rights activists are a type of terrorist. Ben (Roger Panaman) disagrees. Do you think animal rights activists should be considered terrorists? Why or why not?

2. Jill Filipovic and James Kirchick consider whether extreme pro-life groups are responsible for the murder of George Tiller, one of a few doctors willing to perform late-term abortions. Do you think the groups were responsible for Tiller's murder, or was the murder the sole responsibility of the individual who pulled the trigger? Use the viewpoints to justify your position.

Organizations to Contact

The editors have compiled the following list of organizations concerned with the issues presented in this book. The descriptions are derived from materials provided by the organizations. All have publications or information available for interested readers. The list was compiled on the date of publication of the present volume; the information provided here may change. Be aware that many organizations take several weeks or longer to respond to inquiries, so allow as much time as possible.

American-Arab Anti-Discrimination Committee (ADC)
1732 Wisconsin Avenue NW, Washington, DC   20007
(202) 244-2990 • fax: (202) 333-3980
e-mail: adc@adc.org
Web site: www.adc.org

The American-Arab Anti-Discrimination Committee (ADC) is a grassroots organization that supports Arab American rights and encourages Arab American participation in American society. It also fights discrimination and hate crimes against Arab Americans. The ADC publishes a series of issue papers and a number of books that can be ordered from its online store.

Anti-Defamation League (ADL)
(202) 452-8310 • fax: (202) 296-2371
Web site: www.adl.org

The Anti-Defamation League was founded in 1913 "to stop the defamation of the Jewish people and to secure justice and fair treatment to all." Now the nation's premier civil rights/ human relations agency, ADL fights anti-Semitism and all forms of bigotry, defends democratic ideals, and protects civil rights for all. ADL works to stop the defamation of Jews and to ensure fair treatment for all U.S. citizens. It publishes a number of free online newsletters, which can be accessed through its Web site.

Association for Women's Rights in Development (AWID)

215 Spadina Avenue, Suite 150,
Toronto, Ontario M5T 2C7 Canada
(416) 594-3773 • fax: (416) 594-0330
e-mail: contact@awid.org
Web site: www.awid.org

The Association for Women's Rights in Development (AWID) is an international, multigenerational, feminist, creative, future-orientated membership organization committed to achieving gender equality, sustainable development, and human rights for all women. Through its initiatives, AWID seeks to strengthen the responses of women's rights activists to the rise of religious fundamentalism across regions and religions; to develop more knowledge and resources on the issue; to foster a deeper and shared understanding of the way religious fundamentalism works, grows, and undermines women's rights; and to share strategies that have been used by women's rights activists to resist and challenge religious fundamentalism. Articles and interviews on these topics are available on AWID's Web site.

Christian Coalition of America

PO Box 37030, Washington, DC   20013-7030
(202) 479-6900
Web site: www.cc.org

The Christian Coalition of America is a conservative grassroots political organization founded by Pat Robertson in 1989. The coalition was founded to give conservative Christians a voice in government. It provides education and political training to the pro-family community. The organization's goals include strengthening the family, protecting innocent human life, and protecting religious freedom. The coalition's Web site includes a blog, relevant news items, and an online newsletter.

Council on American-Islamic Relations (CAIR)

453 New Jersey Avenue SE, Washington, DC   20003
(202) 488-8787 • fax: (202) 488-0833

e-mail: info@cair.com
Web site: www.cair.com

The Council on American-Islamic Relations (CAIR) is a non-profit membership organization dedicated to presenting an Islamic perspective on public policy issues and to challenging the misrepresentation of Islam and Muslims. CAIR fights discrimination against Muslims in America and lobbies political leaders on issues related to Islam and Muslims. Its Web site includes a section on antiterrorist campaigns as well as print and multimedia news on the topic.

Council on Foreign Relations
Harold Pratt House, 58 East Sixty-eighth St.,
New York, NY   10065
(212) 434-9400 • fax: (212) 434-9800
Web site: www.cfr.org

The Council on Foreign Relations is an independent, nonpartisan membership organization, think tank, and publisher dedicated to being a resource for its members, government officials, business executives, journalists, educators and students, civic and religious leaders, and other citizens to help them better understand the world and the foreign policy choices facing the United States and other countries. The council provides information through the publication of books and the periodical *Foreign Affairs*. It sponsors meetings for scholars, U.S. politicians, and global leaders, and it funds research and reports on current foreign policies affecting the world. Homeland security and defense, international peace and security, and terrorism are all topics of concern to the organization. Scholars within the organization have written extensively on these topics. These reports can be found on the organization's Web site.

Earth First!
Web site: www.earthfirst.org

Earth First! is an international movement composed of small, bioregionally based groups. Earth First! believes that the earth's ecology has become seriously degraded, and it advocates direct action, ranging from involvement in the legal process to civil disobedience, to stop the destruction of the environment. The organization publishes the *Earth First! Journal* and links to relevant news items from its Web site.

Human Life International (HLI)

4 Family Life Lane, Front Royal, VA   22630
(800) 549-5433 • fax: (540) 622-6247
e-mail: hli@hli.org
Web site: www.hli.org

Human Life International (HLI) is a pro-life Catholic education and research organization that believes that the fetus is human from the moment of conception. The organization strives to train, organize, and equip pro-life leaders around the world. The organization publishes books, audiotapes, CDs, and DVDs and offers two free e-mail newsletters, *Mission Report* and *Spirit and Life*.

Islamic Circle of North America (ICNA)

166-26 Eighty-ninth Avenue, Jamaica, NY   11432
(718) 658-1199 • fax: (718) 658-1255
e-mail: info@icna.org
Web site: www.icna.org

Islamic Circle of North America (ICNA) is an Islamic support organization that seeks to promote the values and duties of the Islamic religion. Its Web site offers a free e-mail newsletter as well as downloads and podcasts relating to Islamic teachings. ICNA's New Jersey chapter maintains the WhyIslam Web site (www.whyislam.org), which offers online and printed resources on Islam, including sections on terrorism and jihad.

MuslimBridges.org

ITA Corp., Temecula, CA   92590
Web site: www.muslimbridges.org

MuslimBridges.org is a Web site of ITA Corp., a faith-based nonprofit corporation that also sponsors MuslimChannels.tv. The organization's mission is to build bridges by promoting peace and dialogue through proactive interactions at individual and organizational levels and to provide answers to questions to correct misconceptions of Islam and American Muslims. The Web site has sections on terrorism, suicide bombing, and jihad.

National Abortion Federation (NAF)

1660 L Street NW, Suite 450, Washington, DC   20036
(202) 667-5881 • fax: (202) 667-5890
e-mail: naf@prochoice.org
Web site: www.prochoice.org

The National Abortion Federation (NAF) is a forum for providers of abortion services and others committed to making safe, legal abortions accessible to all women. The organization provides information on abortion services as well as on violence at abortion clinics. NAF publishes educational fact sheets and bulletins on abortion and offers additional materials on its Web site.

Operation Rescue

PO Box 782888, Wichita, KS   67278-2888
(316) 683-6790 • fax: (916) 244-2636
e-mail: info@operationrescue.org
Web site: www.operationrescue.org

Operation Rescue, one of the leading pro-life Christian activist organizations in the United States, conducts abortion clinic demonstrations in large cities across the country. It pickets abortion clinics, stages clinic blockades, and offers sidewalk counseling in the attempt to persuade women not to have abortions. A variety of pro-life publications are available on its Web site.

People for the American Way

2000 M Street NW, Suite 400, Washington, DC   20036
(202) 467-4999
e-mail: pfaw@pfaw.org
Web site: www.pfaw.org

People for the American Way opposes the political agenda of the religious Right. Through public education, lobbying, and legal advocacy, the organization works to defend equal rights. It offers a variety of information on its Web site including a list of right-wing organizations and the blog Right Wing Watch.

People for the Ethical Treatment of Animals (PETA)

501 Front Street, Norfolk, VA   23510
(757) 622-7382
Web site: www.peta.org

An international animal rights organization, People for the Ethical Treatment of Animals (PETA) is dedicated to establishing and protecting the rights of all animals. It focuses on four areas: factory farms, research laboratories, the fur trade, and the entertainment industry. PETA conducts frequent public actions and demonstrations to promote its cause. The organization has a television station, Animal Rights TV; a blog, the PETA Files; and a wide variety of other information available on its Web site.

Planned Parenthood Federation of America

434 West Thirty-third Street, New York, NY   10001
(212) 541-7800 • fax: (212) 245-1845
Web site: www.plannedparenthood.org

Planned Parenthood Federation of America is a national organization that supports women's right to make their own reproductive decisions without governmental interference. It provides contraceptive counseling and services at clinics located throughout the United States. Planned Parenthood's Web site presents a variety of articles, press releases, videos, and medically accurate information about sexual health.

Quilliam

PO Box 60380, London   WC 1A 9AZ England
+44 (0) 207 182 7280 • fax: +44 (0) 207 637 4944

e-mail: information@quilliamfoundation.org
Web site: www.quilliamfoundation.org

Quilliam is a counter-extremism think tank located in London. The founders are former leading ideologues of extremist Islamist organizations based in the United Kingdom—organizations that are still active today. Quilliam aims to use informed and inclusive discussions to counter the Islamist ideology behind terrorism, while simultaneously providing evidence-based recommendations to governments for related policy measures. The organization produces a number of publications, which are available on its Web site.

Southern Poverty Law Center (SPLC)
400 Washington Avenue, Montgomery, AL 36104
(334) 956-8200
Web site: www.splcenter.org

The Southern Poverty Law Center (SPLC) fights discrimination and racism throughout America. Its Intelligence Project monitors hate groups throughout the United States and reports on individual acts of ethnic or racially based violence. SPLC's Web site contains information on a variety of types of hateful extremism.

U.S. Department of Justice (DOJ)
950 Pennsylvania Avenue NW, Washington, DC 20530-0001
(202) 514-2000
e-mail: AskDOJ@usdoj.gov
Web site: www.usdoj.gov

The Department of Justice (DOJ) is the office of the U.S. government charged with upholding the laws of the United States to protect the country and all American citizens. Additionally, the department is responsible for ensuring that all Americans receive fair and impartial judgment in line with the guarantees of the Constitution. Within the DOJ, Joint Terrorism Task Forces (JTTFs) work both on a local and national level to ensure that terrorism does not proliferate within individual communities in the United States. Further information on the activities of both the JTTFs and the DOJ are available on the department's Web site.

Bibliography of Books

Patricia
Baird-Windle and
Eleanor J. Bader

Targets of Hatred: Anti-Abortion Terrorism. New York: Palgrave for St. Martin's Press, 2001.

Richard A. Clarke
and Robert Knake

Cyber War: The Next Threat to National Security and What to Do About It. New York: HarperCollins, 2010.

David Cook and
Olivia Allison

Understanding and Addressing Suicide Attacks: The Faith and Politics of Martyrdom Operations. Westport, CT: Praeger Security International, 2007.

Gregory M. Davis

Religion of Peace? Islam's War Against the World. Los Angeles: World Ahead Pub., 2006.

Ariel Glucklich

Dying for Heaven: Holy Pleasure and Suicide Bombers—Why the Best Qualities of Religion Are Also Its Most Dangerous. New York: HarperOne, 2009.

Michelle
Goldberg

Kingdom Coming: The Rise of Christian Nationalism. New York: W.W. Norton & Co., 2006.

Al Gore

The Assault on Reason. New York: Penguin Press, 2007.

Chris Hedges

American Fascists: The Christian Right and the War on America. New York: Free Press, 2006.

Ed Husain   *The Islamist: Why I Joined Radical Islam in Britain, What I Saw Inside and Why I Left.* London: Penguin, 2007.

Cheryl R. Jorgensen-Earp   *In the Wake of Violence: Image & Social Reform.* East Lansing: Michigan State University Press, 2008.

Mark Juergensmeyer   *Terror in the Mind of God: The Global Rise of Religious Violence.* Berkeley: University of California Press, 2003.

Charles Kimball   *When Religion Becomes Evil: Five Warning Signs.* New York: HarperOne, 2008.

Michael Lerner   *The Left Hand of God: Taking Back Our Country from the Religious Right.* San Francisco, CA: HarperSanFrancisco, 2006.

Donald R. Liddick   *Eco-Terrorism: Radical Environmental and Animal Liberation Movements.* Westport, CT: Praeger, 2006.

Gabriele Marranci   *Understanding Muslim Identity: Rethinking Fundamentalism.* New York: Palgrave Macmillan, 2009.

Gary E. McCuen, ed.   *Abortion: Violence & Extremism.* Hudson, WI: Gary E. McCuen Publications, 1997.

Alister E. McGrath and Joanna Collicutt McGrath   *The Dawkins Delusion: Atheist Fundamentalism and the Denial of the Divine.* Downers Grove, IL: InterVarsity Press, 2007.

Jon Pahl   *Empire of Sacrifice: The Religious Origins of American Violence.* New York: New York University Press, 2010.

Norman   *World War IV: The Long Struggle*
Podhoretz   *Against Islamofascism.* New York: Doubleday, 2007.

Anne Sofie Roald   *Women in Islam: The Western Experience.* New York: Routledge, 2001.

Jens Rydgren, ed.   *Movements of Exclusion: Radical Right-Wing Populism in the Western World.* New York: Nova Science Publishers, 2005.

Frank Schaeffer   *Crazy for God: How I Grew Up as One of the Elect, Helped Found the Religious Right, and Lived to Take All (or Almost All) of It Back.* New York, Carroll & Graf, 2007.

Solomon   *The Tenacity of Unreasonable Beliefs:*
Schimmel   *Fundamentalism and the Fear of Truth.* Oxford: Oxford University Press, 2008.

Charles Selengut   *Sacred Fury: Understanding Religious Violence.* Lanham, MD: Rowman & Littlefield Publishers, 2008.

Jeff Sharlet   *The Family: The Secret Fundamentalism at the Heart of American Power.* New York: Harper Perennial, 2009.

Walid Shoebat   *Why I Left Jihad: The Root of*
                   Terrorism and the Rise of Islam. Ed.
                   June S. Neal. United States: Top
                   Executive Media, 2005.

Dicky Sofjan   *Why Muslims Participate in Jihad: An*
                   Empirical Survey on Islamic Religiosity
                   in Indonesia and Iran. Bandung,
                   Indonesia: Mizan, 2006.

Ron Suskind   *The Way of the World: A Story of*
                   Truth and Hope in an Age of
                   Extremism. New York: Harper
                   Perennial, 2009.

Matt Taibbi   *The Great Derangement: A Terrifying*
                   True Story of War, Politics, and
                   Religion at the Twilight of the
                   American Empire. New York: Spiegel
                   & Grau, 2008.

Gabriel Weimann   *Terror on the Internet: The New*
                   Arena, the New Challenges.
                   Washington, DC: United States
                   Institute of Peace Press, 2006.

Index